Bhutan

Everything You Need to Know

Introduction to the Kingdom of Bhutan

In the heart of the Himalayas, there lies a kingdom unlike any other, a land shrouded in mystique and untouched by the relentless march of time. Welcome to Bhutan, the Land of the Thunder Dragon. Nestled between the giants of India and China, this enchanting realm is a testament to the resilience of culture, nature, and tradition in a rapidly changing world.

Bhutan, often referred to as Druk Yul, the Land of the Thunder Dragon, is a small, landlocked nation in South Asia, situated in the Eastern Himalayas. It is bordered by China to the north and northwest and by India to the south, east, and west. With a population of just over 750,000 people, Bhutan's size may be modest, but its cultural richness and natural beauty are nothing short of extraordinary.

The kingdom of Bhutan, a constitutional monarchy, has a history that spans centuries. While its early origins remain shrouded in mystery, Bhutan's historical narrative is punctuated by the unification of various regions into a cohesive nation. This process began in the 17th century under the leadership of Zhabdrung Ngawang Namgyal, a charismatic figure who played a pivotal role in establishing Bhutan as a distinct political and cultural entity.

One of the defining features of Bhutan is its unwavering commitment to preserving its unique cultural heritage and traditions. Bhutanese culture is deeply influenced by Buddhism, with the majority of the population adhering to the Drukpa Kagyu school of Mahayana Buddhism. This spiritual influence permeates every aspect of life in Bhutan, from the intricate architecture of its monasteries to the colorful festivals that punctuate the Bhutanese calendar. At the heart of Bhutanese culture is the concept of Gross National Happiness (GNH), a holistic approach to development that prioritizes the well-being and happiness of its citizens over economic growth alone. This unique ideology reflects Bhutan's commitment to maintaining a delicate balance between modernization and cultural preservation.

Bhutan's geographic diversity is as astounding as its cultural heritage. From the rugged peaks of the Himalayas to the lush subtropical plains, Bhutan boasts a breathtaking array of landscapes. The country's towering mountains, including the sacred Jomolhari and Jichu Drake peaks, offer some of the most challenging trekking routes in the world.

Nature thrives here, with pristine forests covering over 70% of the land, providing sanctuary to a diverse range of wildlife, including the elusive snow leopard and the endangered Bengal tiger. Bhutan's conservation efforts have been commendable, as it strives to maintain this natural balance while pursuing sustainable development.

The kingdom's commitment to sustainability extends to its unique policy of maintaining a carbon-neutral status. Bhutan is one of the few countries in the world that absorbs more carbon dioxide through its lush forests than it emits, making it a beacon of environmental responsibility.

As we embark on this journey to unravel the mysteries of Bhutan, we will explore its history, culture, natural wonders, and the enduring spirit of its people. Together, we will discover the intricate tapestry that is the Kingdom of Bhutan, where tradition and modernity dance in harmonious balance, and where the pursuit of happiness is not just an ideal but a way of life.

Bhutan's Geographic Overview

Bhutan, nestled in the heart of the Eastern Himalayas, offers a geographic tapestry as diverse as it is awe-inspiring. This landlocked kingdom, often referred to as the "Last Shangri-La," is a place where nature reigns supreme, and its geographical features paint a vivid picture of its unique charm.

To begin with, Bhutan's position on the world map places it between two giants: China to the north and northwest and India to the south, east, and west. This strategic location has not only influenced its history and culture but has also contributed to the nation's distinctive geographical characteristics.

The most striking feature of Bhutan's geography is its dramatic topography. Rugged mountains dominate the landscape, with the mighty Himalayan range running through its northern border. Within this range, Bhutan boasts some of the world's highest peaks, including Gangkhar Puensum, which stands as the tallest unclimbed mountain on the planet. These towering peaks, covered in snow and ice, create not only breathtaking vistas but also some of the most challenging terrain for mountaineers and trekkers.

South of the Himalayas, the terrain descends into deep valleys and rolling hills. These valleys are lush and fertile, providing a stark contrast to the harsh mountain landscapes. The Paro Valley, in particular, is renowned for its picturesque beauty and is home to the nation's only international airport.

Bhutan is crisscrossed by numerous rivers and streams, with the major ones being the Paro Chhu, Wang Chhu, and Punatsang Chhu. These waterways play a vital role in the country's agriculture and hydroelectric power generation.

One cannot talk about Bhutan's geography without mentioning its dense forests. Covering more than 70% of the country, these forests are not only a source of natural beauty but also home to a rich variety of flora and fauna. Bhutan's commitment to preserving its environment is evident in its stringent conservation policies.

Moving from south to north, the country's climate varies significantly. The southern regions experience a subtropical climate with high humidity, while the northern areas, due to their elevation, have a much cooler, alpine climate. These climatic variations have a profound impact on the country's biodiversity, supporting a wide range of species, from tropical plants and animals to cold-adapted creatures.

In summary, Bhutan's geographic overview showcases a land of extremes and contrasts. It is a nation defined by towering peaks, deep valleys, pristine rivers, and dense forests. This remarkable landscape, combined with the nation's commitment to environmental conservation, sets the stage for the unique experiences and adventures that await those who venture into this enchanting realm in the heart of the Himalayas.

Bhutan's Early History and Origins

Bhutan's early history and origins are shrouded in the mists of time, a tapestry woven with threads of legend and historical fragments. This kingdom, hidden away in the Eastern Himalayas, has a rich and enigmatic past that predates recorded history.

Scholars and historians have long grappled with the task of unraveling Bhutan's early history, and while there is no single definitive narrative, there are intriguing pieces of the puzzle that offer glimpses into its ancient origins.

One of the most enduring aspects of Bhutan's early history is its legendary beginnings. According to Bhutanese mythology, the kingdom's origins can be traced back to the arrival of the saintly figure, Guru Rinpoche, also known as Padmasambhava. It is said that he brought Buddhism to Bhutan in the 8th century and played a pivotal role in shaping the country's religious and cultural identity. The influence of Guru Rinpoche remains strong to this day, with his legacy evident in the numerous monasteries and temples that dot the Bhutanese landscape.

Another key figure in Bhutan's early history is Zhabdrung Ngawang Namgyal, a charismatic leader who unified Bhutan in the 17th century. His arrival marked a turning point in the nation's history, as he established a theocratic government and laid the foundations for Bhutanese culture and governance that endure to this day.

Archaeological discoveries have shed light on Bhutan's ancient past as well. Ruins and artifacts unearthed in various parts of the country provide evidence of early human habitation dating back to the Neolithic period. These findings hint at a long and complex history of human settlement in Bhutan.

The region's geographical location has also played a significant role in its history. Bhutan's proximity to Tibet and India meant that it was influenced by the cultural and political dynamics of both regions. Over the centuries, it became a buffer state between these two powers, with Bhutanese rulers often forging alliances with neighboring Tibetan and Indian leaders.

While the early history of Bhutan remains shrouded in mystery, it is clear that the kingdom's origins are deeply intertwined with Buddhism, legendary figures like Guru Rinpoche, and the visionary leadership of Zhabdrung Ngawang Namgyal. These elements have left an indelible mark on Bhutan's cultural, religious, and political identity, shaping it into the unique and enchanting kingdom that it is today.

The Unification of Bhutan

The Unification of Bhutan marks a pivotal chapter in the nation's history, a saga of political intrigue, visionary leadership, and the forging of a distinct identity. Bhutan, nestled in the Eastern Himalayas, was once a patchwork of warring territories and feuding clans. It was during the 17th century that this fragmented land began to coalesce into a unified kingdom under the guidance of a charismatic figure named Zhabdrung Ngawang Namgyal.

Zhabdrung Ngawang Namgyal, a revered spiritual leader and military strategist, arrived in Bhutan in the early 17th century, bringing with him the teachings of Tibetan Buddhism. His presence marked a turning point in the region's history. He not only played a pivotal role in propagating Buddhism but also laid the foundations for a unified Bhutan.

One of Zhabdrung's key accomplishments was the establishment of a theocratic government. He created a system of governance that combined both religious and secular authority, with himself as the spiritual and temporal leader. This system, known as the dual system of government, endured for centuries and played a central role in Bhutanese politics.

Zhabdrung was also a visionary architect and builder. He constructed numerous dzongs, fortified monastic complexes that served as centers of administration, religion, and defense. These dzongs, with their distinctive architecture and strategic locations, became enduring symbols of Bhutan's unity and strength.

The unification of Bhutan was not without its challenges. Zhabdrung faced opposition from rival religious and political factions. His military campaigns to consolidate power and unify the region were marked by both triumphs and setbacks. Nevertheless, his determination and strategic acumen ultimately prevailed, and he succeeded in bringing most of Bhutan's disparate territories under his rule.

The legacy of Zhabdrung Ngawang Namgyal endures to this day. His influence on Bhutanese culture, religion, and governance is immeasurable. His unification efforts laid the groundwork for the Bhutanese state, forging a sense of national identity that transcended regional divisions.

The dual system of government, established by Zhabdrung, remained in place until the early 20th century when Bhutan underwent significant political reforms. The institution of monarchy became the central authority, and Bhutan transitioned into a constitutional monarchy in 2008.

The unification of Bhutan was a complex and multifaceted process, driven by the vision and determination of Zhabdrung Ngawang Namgyal. His legacy lives on in the kingdom's enduring traditions, its dzongs, and its unique blend of Buddhism and governance. Bhutan's journey from fragmentation to unification is a testament to the resilience and unity of its people.

The Arrival of Buddhism in Bhutan

The Arrival of Buddhism in Bhutan is a pivotal chapter in the country's history, one that has left an indelible mark on its culture, spirituality, and way of life. This ancient Himalayan kingdom, nestled between India and Tibet, was once steeped in animistic and indigenous beliefs, but the arrival of Buddhism in Bhutan heralded a profound transformation.

Buddhism made its way into Bhutan in the 8th century, with the arrival of Guru Rinpoche, also known as Padmasambhava. This revered figure, considered the second Buddha, played a central role in introducing Buddhism to the region. Legend has it that Guru Rinpoche flew to Bhutan on the back of a tigress, a story that symbolizes the triumph of Buddhism over the indigenous beliefs.

Guru Rinpoche's teachings and spiritual prowess had a profound impact on the Bhutanese people. He not only propagated Buddhism but also tamed the spirits and deities that were integral to the pre-Buddhist Bon religion. His influence extended beyond religious matters; he became an instrumental figure in Bhutanese politics, helping establish a unified and harmonious society.

One of the enduring legacies of Guru Rinpoche's arrival is the construction of Bhutan's many monasteries and temples. These spiritual sanctuaries, known as gompas, are scattered across the Bhutanese landscape. They serve as centers of worship, learning, and cultural preservation, and are often set amidst breathtaking natural settings, harmonizing spirituality with the surrounding environment.

The form of Buddhism that took root in Bhutan is known as Vajrayana or Tantric Buddhism. This branch of Buddhism emphasizes esoteric practices, meditation, and rituals. It became deeply intertwined with Bhutanese culture, influencing everything from art and architecture to daily life and governance.

Bhutan's Buddhist heritage is also reflected in its unique religious festivals, or tsechus. These vibrant celebrations, often featuring masked dances and religious pageantry, are held throughout the year and draw thousands of Bhutanese and tourists alike. The most famous of these festivals is the Paro Tsechu, which celebrates Guru Rinpoche's arrival in Bhutan.

The arrival of Buddhism in Bhutan not only transformed the spiritual landscape but also played a significant role in the nation's unification. It provided a common cultural and religious thread that bound together the diverse regions and ethnic groups within the country.

Today, Bhutan's commitment to Buddhism remains unwavering. The majority of its population adheres to the Drukpa Kagyu school of Mahayana Buddhism, and the influence of Guru Rinpoche continues to permeate every facet of Bhutanese life, from its festivals and rituals to its approach to governance and Gross National Happiness.

The arrival of Buddhism in Bhutan was not merely a historical event; it was a transformative force that shaped the nation's identity and continues to guide its path towards spiritual fulfillment and cultural preservation.

Bhutan's Dynastic History

Bhutan's dynastic history is a rich and intricate tapestry that weaves together the stories of the various royal families that have ruled this Himalayan kingdom over the centuries. This history is marked by a succession of dynasties, each leaving its unique imprint on the nation's governance and culture.

The early history of Bhutan was characterized by fragmentation and regionalism, with different regions and principalities ruled by local leaders. It was not until the arrival of Zhabdrung Ngawang Namgyal in the 17th century that Bhutan began to coalesce into a unified kingdom. Zhabdrung's reign marked the establishment of the first Bhutanese theocratic state, with him serving as both the spiritual and temporal leader.

Following Zhabdrung Ngawang Namgyal's death, Bhutan entered a period of instability marked by internal conflicts and external threats. This era saw the rise of regional leaders and the disintegration of central authority. The Bhutanese ruling elite struggled to maintain unity and political control.

In the 19th century, Bhutan faced significant challenges from neighboring British India. The Bhutan War of 1864-1865 resulted in the Treaty of Sinchula, which established British influence in Bhutan while recognizing its internal autonomy. During this period, Bhutan maintained a system of dual governance with both religious and secular leaders.

The late 19th century witnessed the emergence of a new Bhutanese dynasty. Ugyen Wangchuck, a charismatic leader, successfully unified Bhutan under his rule. He was crowned as the first hereditary monarch in 1907, marking the beginning of the Wangchuck dynasty, which continues to rule Bhutan to this day.

Under the leadership of the Wangchuck dynasty, Bhutan underwent a series of reforms aimed at modernizing the country while preserving its unique culture and traditions. The reign of King Jigme Dorji Wangchuck in the mid-20th century saw the introduction of democratic reforms and the establishment of a National Assembly.

King Jigme Singye Wangchuck, who succeeded his father, King Jigme Dorji Wangchuck, in 1972, introduced the concept of Gross National Happiness (GNH) as a guiding principle for Bhutan's development. His reign marked a period of significant political and economic transformation while emphasizing the importance of cultural preservation and environmental conservation.

In 2008, Bhutan made a historic transition to a constitutional monarchy with the first democratic elections and the crowning of King Jigme Khesar Namgyel Wangchuck. This transition marked a new chapter in Bhutan's history, combining traditional monarchy with modern democratic governance.

Bhutan's dynastic history is a testament to the resilience and adaptability of its people and leaders. The Wangchuck dynasty's commitment to balancing modernization with the preservation of cultural heritage and the environment reflects the ongoing evolution of this unique Himalayan kingdom.

Bhutan's Transition to a Constitutional Monarchy

Bhutan's transition to a constitutional monarchy is a remarkable chapter in the nation's history, a story of modernization, democracy, and the preservation of cultural heritage. This journey from absolute monarchy to constitutional monarchy reflects Bhutan's commitment to adapting to the changing world while safeguarding its unique identity.

The roots of this transition can be traced back to the mid-20th century. During the reign of King Jigme Dorji Wangchuck in the 1950s and 1960s, Bhutan saw a series of transformative reforms. King Jigme Dorji Wangchuck initiated changes aimed at modernizing the country's infrastructure, education system, and economy. These reforms were driven by a vision of improving the lives of Bhutanese citizens and ensuring the nation's sustainability.

One of the most significant milestones in Bhutan's journey toward a constitutional monarchy was the promulgation of the first constitution in 1953. This document, known as the "National Law of Bhutan," laid the groundwork for a modern legal and administrative framework. It also introduced the concept of "Druk Gyalpo," or Dragon King, which became the official title for Bhutan's monarchs.

The reign of King Jigme Singye Wangchuck, who succeeded his father in 1972, marked a pivotal period in Bhutan's transition. He continued the modernization efforts and introduced democratic reforms. In 1998, he voluntarily relinquished absolute power and transferred it to the Council of Ministers, marking the beginning of a constitutional form of government.

In 2008, Bhutan held its first-ever democratic elections, a historic moment that culminated in the crowning of King Jigme Khesar Namgyel Wangchuck. The newly adopted constitution established a parliamentary democracy, with a bicameral legislature consisting of the National Assembly and the National Council. It also outlined the powers and responsibilities of the monarchy, ensuring a harmonious balance between traditional governance and democratic principles.

The transition to a constitutional monarchy was accompanied by the introduction of Gross National Happiness (GNH) as a guiding philosophy for Bhutan's development. GNH emphasizes the well-being and happiness of Bhutanese citizens over purely economic growth, reflecting the nation's commitment to holistic development.

Bhutan's path to constitutional monarchy has not been without its challenges and adjustments. However, it stands as a testament to the nation's ability to adapt to the changing global landscape while preserving its rich cultural heritage and unique traditions. The Bhutanese people have embraced democracy while continuing to honor their monarchy, striking a balance that is both forward-looking and deeply rooted in their history and values.

Bhutan's Political Structure and Leadership

Bhutan's political structure and leadership are characterized by a unique blend of traditional monarchy and modern democratic governance. This distinctive system has evolved over the years, reflecting the nation's commitment to preserving its cultural heritage while embracing contemporary principles of government.

At the heart of Bhutan's political structure is the monarchy. The King of Bhutan, who holds the title of Druk Gyalpo, is the head of state and plays a pivotal role in the nation's governance. The monarchy in Bhutan is hereditary, with a line of kings from the Wangchuck dynasty, dating back to King Ugyen Wangchuck, who was crowned in 1907. The monarchy is deeply respected and revered by the Bhutanese people, and the king's role goes beyond symbolic; it includes involvement in important national matters.

In addition to the monarchy, Bhutan's political system incorporates democratic elements. The country transitioned to a constitutional monarchy in 2008 with the adoption of its first constitution. This marked a significant step towards embracing modern democratic principles. Bhutan's constitution establishes a parliamentary democracy, with a bicameral legislature consisting of the National Assembly and the National Council.

The National Assembly, known as the Gyelyong Tshogde, is the lower house of Bhutan's parliament. Its members are elected by the people in a democratic voting process. The National Assembly plays a vital role in crafting and passing legislation, addressing policy matters, and representing the interests of Bhutanese citizens.

The National Council, or Gyelyong Tshogdu, is the upper house of parliament. Its members are not elected by the public but are instead chosen by local leaders, religious bodies, and the king. The National Council serves as a forum for reviewing and revising legislation proposed by the National Assembly. It also plays a role in safeguarding Bhutan's cultural and traditional values.

Bhutan's executive branch is headed by the Prime Minister, known as the Lyonchhen. The Prime Minister is the head of government and is responsible for overseeing the day-to-day administration of the country. The King appoints the Prime Minister, who is usually the leader of the political party that wins the majority of seats in the National Assembly.

Bhutan's political landscape is characterized by a multi-party system. Political parties participate in democratic elections, and the party with the majority of seats in the National Assembly forms the government. Bhutan's political parties advocate various policies and platforms, reflecting the diversity of opinions and ideas within the nation.

Overall, Bhutan's political structure and leadership reflect a harmonious synthesis of traditional monarchy and modern democracy. This unique approach allows Bhutan to preserve its cultural heritage while embracing the principles of representative government and citizen participation. It is a testament to Bhutan's commitment to balancing tradition with progress in its quest for Gross National Happiness and holistic development.

The Gross National Happiness Index

The Gross National Happiness Index, often abbreviated as GNH, is a distinctive and innovative approach to measuring the well-being and happiness of a nation's citizens. It's a concept that sets Bhutan apart from most other countries, emphasizing quality of life and happiness over mere economic indicators.

This unique measure was introduced in Bhutan in the 1970s under the leadership of King Jigme Singye Wangchuck. It reflects the nation's commitment to ensuring that development benefits its citizens in ways that go beyond traditional measures like Gross Domestic Product (GDP). Bhutan's leaders recognized that economic growth alone does not guarantee the well-being and happiness of its people.

The GNH Index is a holistic framework that encompasses nine domains, each contributing to a comprehensive assessment of well-being. These domains include psychological well-being, health, education, time use, cultural diversity and resilience, good governance, community vitality, ecological diversity and resilience, and living standards.

Within these domains, numerous indicators are used to assess the well-being and happiness of Bhutanese citizens. For example, in the domain of psychological well-being, factors like the prevalence of positive and negative emotions are considered. In the health domain, indicators related to access to healthcare and health outcomes are evaluated. Education is measured through factors such as literacy rates and access to quality education.

The GNH Index is not just a theoretical framework; it's put into practice through regular surveys and assessments of Bhutanese citizens. The government actively seeks the input of its people to understand their levels of happiness and well-being. This data helps guide policy decisions and ensure that government initiatives are aligned with the goal of enhancing the overall quality of life in Bhutan.

One of the fundamental principles underlying the GNH Index is the belief that material and spiritual well-being are interrelated. Bhutan recognizes that cultural preservation, environmental conservation, and good governance are all integral components of happiness. By focusing on these aspects, the country seeks to create a balanced and sustainable approach to development.

The GNH Index has garnered international attention and praise for its innovative approach to measuring well-being. It offers a model that challenges the conventional wisdom that economic growth is the sole indicator of a nation's success. Bhutan's commitment to Gross National Happiness demonstrates its dedication to the overall well-being and contentment of its citizens.

In conclusion, the Gross National Happiness Index is a pioneering concept that embodies Bhutan's unique approach to governance and development. It reflects a deep commitment to the happiness and well-being of its people, and it continues to be a source of inspiration and admiration worldwide as it offers an alternative vision for the future of nations beyond GDP-focused measures.

Bhutan's Economy and Development

Bhutan's economy and development have been shaped by its commitment to Gross National Happiness (GNH) and its unique approach to balancing economic growth with cultural preservation and environmental conservation. This Himalayan kingdom, nestled between India and China, has embraced a sustainable and holistic model of development that places the well-being of its citizens at the forefront.

Bhutan's economy has traditionally been agrarian, with the majority of its population engaged in subsistence farming. Rice, maize, barley, and wheat are some of the staple crops grown in the fertile valleys. Livestock, including yak and cattle, are also crucial to the livelihoods of many Bhutanese.

Over the years, Bhutan has witnessed significant economic diversification, driven by government initiatives aimed at reducing the country's reliance on agriculture. Hydroelectric power generation has become a cornerstone of Bhutan's economy. The nation's fast-flowing rivers and abundant water resources provide the ideal conditions for hydropower projects. Electricity generated by these projects is not only sufficient to meet domestic needs but is also a valuable export commodity, primarily to India.

Tourism is another sector that has gained prominence in Bhutan's economy. The government has adopted a unique "High-Value, Low-Impact" tourism policy, which focuses on attracting a limited number of high-end tourists while preserving the country's natural and cultural heritage. This approach ensures that tourism contributes to Bhutan's economic development without compromising its pristine environment.

The sustainable development model in Bhutan extends to environmental conservation. The country is committed to maintaining a carbon-neutral status, and its constitution mandates that a minimum of 60% of its land must remain forested. These efforts align with Bhutan's broader goal of preserving its unique biodiversity and ensuring that its natural resources are used in a sustainable manner.

Bhutan's development journey has also emphasized education and healthcare. The government has made significant investments in these sectors to improve the quality of life for its citizens. Education is free up to the secondary level, and healthcare services are accessible to all Bhutanese, contributing to improved human development indicators.

In recent years, Bhutan has pursued economic self-reliance and diversification through initiatives such as agriculture modernization, small and medium-sized enterprise development, and the promotion of industries like information technology and renewable energy.

The nation's commitment to Gross National Happiness has provided a guiding philosophy for development. It emphasizes not only economic well-being but also cultural preservation, good governance, and community vitality. Bhutan's development approach serves as a model for other nations seeking a balanced and sustainable path to progress.

In conclusion, Bhutan's economy and development reflect a commitment to holistic well-being and environmental stewardship. The nation's unique approach, guided by the principles of Gross National Happiness, demonstrates that economic growth can be achieved while preserving culture, protecting the environment, and prioritizing the happiness and well-being of its people.

Bhutan's Education System

Bhutan's education system is a cornerstone of its development efforts and reflects the nation's commitment to fostering knowledge, skills, and cultural preservation among its citizens. This Himalayan kingdom places a strong emphasis on education as a means to empower its people and promote Gross National Happiness (GNH).

The Bhutanese education system is organized into several levels, including preschool, primary, secondary, and tertiary education. Education is compulsory for children up to the age of 14, ensuring that a strong foundation is laid for every Bhutanese child.

Preschool education, while not mandatory, is available to prepare young children for formal schooling. Primary education begins at age six and extends for six years, providing a basic education in subjects such as language, mathematics, science, and social studies. The curriculum also incorporates elements of Bhutanese culture, history, and values.

Secondary education in Bhutan spans six years and is divided into two cycles: lower secondary and higher secondary. The lower secondary cycle introduces a broader range of subjects and builds on the foundation laid in primary school. Students then progress to higher secondary education, where they have the opportunity to choose from various streams, including science, commerce, and arts, based on their interests and career aspirations.

Bhutan places a strong emphasis on ensuring that education is accessible to all its citizens, regardless of their geographical location. Schools are distributed across the country, including in remote and rural areas, to ensure that even the most isolated communities have access to quality education.

One of the distinctive features of Bhutan's education system is its integration of GNH principles. While academic subjects are crucial, the curriculum also emphasizes the importance of character development, values, and ethics. This holistic approach is intended to produce well-rounded individuals who not only excel academically but also contribute positively to their communities and society.

Furthermore, Bhutan's education system places an emphasis on cultural preservation and the promotion of the national language, Dzongkha. Bhutanese history, culture, and traditions are woven into the curriculum, ensuring that the younger generations continue to embrace their heritage.

Tertiary education in Bhutan is provided by institutions such as the Royal University of Bhutan (RUB) and other colleges. These institutions offer a range of undergraduate and postgraduate programs, allowing Bhutanese students to pursue higher education without leaving the country.

In conclusion, Bhutan's education system is a vital component of the nation's development strategy. It aims to empower its citizens with knowledge, skills, and a deep sense of cultural identity while aligning with the principles of GNH. This commitment to holistic education is an integral part of Bhutan's vision for a prosperous and happy society.

Bhutanese Arts and Crafts

Bhutanese arts and crafts are a testament to the nation's rich cultural heritage and creative traditions that have thrived for centuries. The artistic expressions of this Himalayan kingdom are deeply intertwined with its religious beliefs, history, and way of life.

One of the most iconic forms of Bhutanese art is thangka painting. Thangkas are intricate, scroll-like paintings that often depict deities, religious figures, and scenes from Buddhist mythology. These works of art serve not only as spiritual objects but also as a means of preserving and conveying religious teachings. The intricate detail and vibrant colors of thangkas are a testament to the skill and devotion of Bhutanese artists.

Another prominent artistic tradition in Bhutan is statue making. Skilled artisans carve intricate statues of Buddhas, Bodhisattvas, and other religious figures from wood, stone, and metal. These statues are often enshrined in temples and monasteries, adding to the spiritual ambiance of these sacred spaces.

Bhutan is also known for its vibrant textile industry. The country's weavers produce intricately patterned fabrics using traditional weaving techniques passed down through generations. The most famous textile product is the kira and gho, the traditional attire for Bhutanese women and men, respectively. These garments are not only functional but also works of art, with designs that vary by region and hold cultural significance.

The art of woodcarving is another integral part of Bhutanese craftsmanship. Elaborate wooden facades, intricate window frames, and finely carved altar pieces can be found in monasteries, temples, and traditional Bhutanese architecture. The motifs often feature religious symbols and mythological creatures.

Bhutanese pottery and ceramics showcase the creativity of the country's artisans. From utilitarian pottery like cooking vessels to decorative ceramics, these pieces reflect Bhutan's artistic diversity. Often, pottery is adorned with vibrant colors and intricate designs inspired by nature and religious themes.

Mask making is yet another vibrant tradition in Bhutanese culture. Masks are used in religious rituals, dances, and festivals. Each mask is a unique work of art, representing various deities, demons, and mythological characters. The masks come to life during colorful and dramatic mask dances performed during religious festivals.

Bhutanese arts and crafts extend beyond these traditional forms to contemporary expressions. Many artists in Bhutan draw inspiration from their cultural heritage and use modern mediums to create innovative and meaningful artwork.

The appreciation and preservation of Bhutanese arts and crafts are integral to the nation's identity and values. The government and cultural institutions actively support and promote these traditions, ensuring that they continue to flourish and contribute to Bhutan's unique cultural landscape.

In conclusion, Bhutanese arts and crafts are a testament to the country's vibrant cultural heritage, with traditions deeply rooted in religion, history, and creativity. These artistic expressions serve not only as cultural treasures but also as a source of pride and identity for the Bhutanese people.

Bhutanese Architecture and Dzongs

Bhutanese architecture and dzongs are integral components of the nation's cultural and historical identity, reflecting both its spiritual heritage and its unique approach to building and design.

Dzongs, in particular, are iconic structures that are not only architectural marvels but also serve as administrative, religious, and defensive centers. These fortress-like buildings are found throughout Bhutan and are characterized by their imposing facades, intricate woodwork, and strategic locations.

One of the most famous dzongs is the Punakha Dzong, which is not only architecturally impressive but also holds historical significance. It served as the capital of Bhutan until the 1950s and is often referred to as the "Palace of Great Happiness." The Punakha Dzong is a stunning example of Bhutanese architecture, with whitewashed walls, golden spires, and beautiful courtyards.

Another notable dzong is the Paro Dzong, which sits on a hill overlooking the Paro Valley. It's a striking structure with a unique design that incorporates both religious and administrative functions. The Paro Dzong is also home to one of Bhutan's most revered relics, the sacred mask dance known as the Paro Tsechu, which attracts thousands of visitors and pilgrims every year.

Dzongs serve as centers of governance, housing the offices of local administrators and monks who oversee religious activities. They are also hubs of cultural and spiritual life, hosting religious festivals, ceremonies, and events that celebrate Bhutanese traditions and beliefs.

The architectural style of dzongs combines elements of Bhutanese and Tibetan design, reflecting the nation's cultural and religious ties to Tibet. They are typically constructed using traditional building techniques, including rammed earth walls, wooden beams, and intricately carved details. The use of local materials and the incorporation of traditional methods contribute to the sustainability and longevity of these structures.

Bhutanese architecture extends beyond dzongs to encompass a wide range of building styles. Traditional Bhutanese houses, often made of mud and timber, feature distinctive sloping roofs and intricate woodwork. These homes reflect the close connection between Bhutanese people and their natural surroundings.

Bhutan's architectural traditions are not confined to the past; they continue to shape the nation's contemporary building practices. Even modern structures incorporate elements of traditional design to maintain a sense of cultural continuity and identity.

In recent years, Bhutan has also embraced environmentally sustainable architecture, with a focus on energy-efficient and eco-friendly construction techniques. This reflects the nation's commitment to environmental conservation and its aspiration to maintain a harmonious relationship between human habitation and nature.

In conclusion, Bhutanese architecture and dzongs are living testaments to the country's rich cultural heritage and unique approach to design and construction. These structures serve as physical embodiments of Bhutan's spiritual and administrative life, and they continue to inspire admiration and awe among both locals and visitors for their beauty and historical significance.

Traditional Bhutanese Dress: Gho and Kira

Traditional Bhutanese dress, comprising the Gho for men and the Kira for women, is not merely clothing; it's a living expression of Bhutan's culture, identity, and heritage. These garments are steeped in history, symbolism, and intricate craftsmanship, representing the nation's enduring commitment to preserving its unique way of life.

The Gho, worn by Bhutanese men, is a knee-length robe secured at the waist with a cloth belt called a kera. This traditional attire is not only practical for Bhutan's mountainous terrain but also a symbol of Bhutanese identity. The Gho is typically made from handwoven fabric, often featuring vibrant patterns and colors that reflect the wearer's social status, age, and region. The sleeves are wide, and the robe allows for ease of movement, making it ideal for both work and daily life.

The Kira, the traditional attire for Bhutanese women, consists of a rectangular piece of cloth wrapped around the body and held in place with a belt known as a koma. The Kira is a symbol of grace and elegance, with a wide variety of fabrics, colors, and patterns to choose from. It can be adorned with intricate brocade patterns and embroidery, making each Kira a unique work of art. The design and color of the Kira may also convey information about the wearer's marital status and regional origin.

Both the Gho and Kira are more than just clothing; they are deeply tied to Bhutan's spiritual and cultural values. The color red, for instance, is considered auspicious and is often featured in both garments. Additionally, the Bhutanese people believe that wearing these traditional dresses brings good luck and protects against negative influences.

The traditional dress is not limited to special occasions; it is the everyday attire for Bhutanese people. It's worn at work, during festivals, while visiting temples and monasteries, and even at government offices. This commitment to preserving traditional dress is enshrined in Bhutanese law, which mandates that citizens wear Gho and Kira during working hours.

The preservation of traditional dress is not just a matter of fashion but a way of safeguarding Bhutan's unique cultural heritage. The Bhutanese government actively promotes the wearing of traditional dress as a means of preserving Bhutanese identity in the face of modernization and globalization.

Moreover, Bhutanese dress is a source of pride and a symbol of unity. It transcends regional and ethnic differences, providing a sense of belonging to a larger Bhutanese community.

In conclusion, traditional Bhutanese dress, consisting of the Gho and Kira, is more than just clothing; it's a living expression of Bhutan's culture, history, and values. These garments are worn with pride and continue to play a central role in preserving the nation's unique identity in a rapidly changing world.

Bhutanese Festivals and Celebrations

Bhutanese festivals and celebrations are vibrant and integral aspects of the nation's cultural tapestry, deeply rooted in religion, tradition, and communal spirit. These festive occasions serve not only as opportunities for merriment but also as a means of fostering a sense of unity, gratitude, and spiritual connection among the Bhutanese people.

One of the most renowned festivals in Bhutan is the Paro Tsechu, celebrated annually in the Paro Dzong in honor of Guru Rinpoche, the patron saint of Bhutan. This grand festival features colorful masked dances and religious performances that depict stories from Buddhist scriptures and offer blessings to the attendees. The Paro Tsechu attracts both locals and tourists alike and is a visual spectacle filled with vibrant costumes, intricate masks, and intricate choreography.

Another significant festival is the Thimphu Tshechu, which takes place in the capital city, Thimphu. This festival coincides with the birthday of Guru Rinpoche and features similar mask dances, along with other religious rituals and cultural performances. The Thimphu Tshechu is a vibrant showcase of Bhutanese culture and spirituality and draws large crowds of devotees and spectators.

The Jambay Lhakhang Drup is a unique festival held in the Bumthang district of Bhutan. It is known for the famous "fire dance," where participants walk barefoot over a path of hot embers. This ancient ritual is believed to purify sins and bring good luck. The festival also includes traditional mask dances and cultural exhibitions, making it a distinctive and spiritually significant event.

Bhutan's festivals are not limited to major celebrations like Tsechus. Many smaller, community-based festivals and rituals take place throughout the year, highlighting the diversity of Bhutanese culture. These local celebrations often involve traditional music, dance, and religious ceremonies that are specific to particular regions or villages.

Losar, the Bhutanese New Year, is another important celebration. It typically occurs in February or March and is marked by prayer ceremonies, family gatherings, and the exchange of gifts. People also engage in traditional games and sports during this festive period.

The Wangdue Phodrang Tshechu, Punakha Drubchen, and Haa Summer Festival are just a few more examples of the many festivals that punctuate Bhutan's calendar, each offering a unique insight into the country's rich cultural traditions and religious practices.

Participation in these festivals is not limited to Bhutanese nationals; visitors are welcomed to join in the celebrations and gain a deeper understanding of Bhutan's culture and spirituality. Festivals are a bridge between the past and the present, connecting Bhutan's ancient traditions with its modern identity.

In conclusion, Bhutanese festivals and celebrations are vibrant expressions of the nation's cultural and spiritual heritage. These events serve as a living testament to Bhutan's commitment to preserving its unique identity and fostering a sense of community, gratitude, and devotion among its people.

The Role of Religion in Bhutanese Life

The role of religion in Bhutanese life is deeply intertwined with the fabric of the nation, influencing every aspect of daily existence, from social customs to governance and art. Bhutan's unique brand of Buddhism, known as Vajrayana Buddhism or Tantric Buddhism, is not merely a belief system; it's a way of life, a moral compass, and a source of profound spiritual connection.

Buddhism was introduced to Bhutan in the 8th century by Guru Padmasambhava, also known as Guru Rinpoche. His teachings and influence left an indelible mark on the country, shaping its religious and cultural identity. Today, Bhutan is the last bastion of Vajrayana Buddhism, and this spiritual tradition is at the heart of the Bhutanese way of life.

The majority of Bhutanese people are devout Buddhists, and their daily routines are punctuated by acts of worship, prayer, and offerings. Monasteries, stupas, and prayer flags adorn the landscape, serving as constant reminders of the spiritual path. The sound of prayer wheels being spun, the chanting of mantras, and the aroma of incense wafting through the air are ubiquitous elements of Bhutanese life.

Monastic institutions, like the central monastic body in Thimphu known as the Central Monk Body, play a significant role in preserving and propagating Buddhism. Monks and nuns are revered members of society, and many Bhutanese families send at least one child to join a monastic institution. These young novices and monks undergo rigorous religious training, studying Buddhist scriptures, philosophy, and meditation techniques.

Bhutan's governance is also influenced by religion. The country's spiritual leader, the Je Khenpo, holds a prominent position and provides guidance on religious matters. Additionally, the king of Bhutan is expected to uphold and protect Buddhism, demonstrating the symbiotic relationship between the monarchy and religion.

Festivals, or Tsechus, are a crucial part of Bhutanese religious life. These celebrations, featuring colorful mask dances and religious rituals, are held throughout the year in various monasteries and dzongs. Tsechus serve as opportunities for spiritual devotion, cultural expression, and community bonding.

The role of religion extends to Bhutan's approach to nature and the environment. The belief in the sanctity of all living beings and the interdependence of humans and nature has led to a strong commitment to environmental conservation. Bhutan is known for its stringent policies on forest preservation, wildlife protection, and sustainability.

Additionally, the concept of Gross National Happiness (GNH), which guides Bhutan's development, is deeply rooted in Buddhist principles. GNH emphasizes well-being, spiritual growth, and environmental sustainability, alongside material progress. It reflects the belief that true happiness arises from inner peace, harmony with nature, and ethical living.

In conclusion, the role of religion in Bhutanese life is profound and all-encompassing. Buddhism permeates every facet of society, from personal beliefs to cultural practices, governance, and environmental stewardship. It is the spiritual cornerstone of Bhutan, shaping its unique identity and guiding its people on a path toward inner and collective well-being.

Bhutanese Cuisine: A Taste of the Himalayas

Bhutanese cuisine is a delightful journey into the flavors of the Himalayas, offering a unique blend of taste, tradition, and culture. The country's culinary heritage is deeply rooted in its history, geography, and Buddhist beliefs, resulting in dishes that are as diverse as the nation's landscapes.

One of the staples of Bhutanese cuisine is rice, which forms the foundation of most meals. The Bhutanese consume red rice, a nutritious and slightly nutty variety, along with white rice. The rice is often accompanied by a wide array of side dishes that showcase the country's culinary creativity.

Chili peppers are a defining feature of Bhutanese cuisine. They are not just an ingredient; they are a cultural icon. Chili peppers are used generously in most dishes, either dried and ground into a fiery spice called "ezay" or added fresh to create intensely spicy flavors. The love for chili peppers is a testament to the Bhutanese people's tolerance for heat and their belief that spicy food wards off evil spirits.

Ema Datshi is perhaps the most famous Bhutanese dish and a true embodiment of the nation's love for chili peppers. It's a spicy concoction of green chili peppers and cheese, typically served with rice. The creamy, fiery blend of flavors makes it a favorite among locals and a must-try for visitors seeking an authentic Bhutanese culinary experience.

Another popular dish is Phaksha Paa, a flavorful pork stew made with succulent chunks of pork belly, dried chilies, and radishes. The dish is slow-cooked to perfection, allowing the flavors to meld together and create a rich, spicy, and hearty meal.

Momos, dumplings stuffed with various fillings like meat, cheese, or vegetables, are a beloved snack and street food in Bhutan. They are often served with a fiery dipping sauce that adds an extra kick to the savory dumplings.

Bhutan's mountainous terrain provides an abundance of fresh vegetables, which are incorporated into many dishes. Mustard greens, spinach, and turnips are commonly used, both for their taste and nutritional value. Dairy products like butter and cheese also feature prominently in Bhutanese cuisine.

Traditional Bhutanese meals often include a variety of side dishes and condiments, such as spicy pickles, sautéed vegetables, and a mild curry known as "shamu datshi," made with mushrooms and cheese.

In recent years, Bhutanese cuisine has begun to embrace international influences, with some restaurants offering a fusion of Bhutanese and Western dishes. However, traditional Bhutanese food remains at the heart of the nation's culinary identity, reflecting its cultural heritage and connection to the land.

Bhutanese cuisine is not just about nourishment; it's a celebration of flavors, traditions, and the country's unique way of life. It offers a tantalizing journey into the heart of the Himalayas, where every dish tells a story of history, culture, and the enduring spirit of the Bhutanese people.

Bhutan's Unique Flora and Fauna

Bhutan's unique flora and fauna are a testament to the country's commitment to environmental conservation and its pristine natural landscapes. Nestled in the heart of the Eastern Himalayas, Bhutan boasts an extraordinary biodiversity that ranges from lush subtropical forests to high-altitude alpine meadows. This chapter explores the remarkable natural heritage that makes Bhutan a haven for biodiversity enthusiasts and nature lovers alike.

The diverse ecosystems of Bhutan include subtropical forests in the south, temperate forests in the central region, and alpine meadows and glaciers in the north. These variations in altitude and climate provide a habitat for a stunning array of plant and animal species.

Bhutan is known for its rich variety of plant life, with over 5,500 species of vascular plants recorded. The country's forests are home to ancient trees, including the Bhutan Fir and the Blue Pine. These forests are not only ecologically significant but also culturally revered, with many trees considered sacred.

Bhutan's national flower, the Blue Poppy (Meconopsis horridula), is a rare and sought-after sight. It blooms in the high-altitude regions of the country and is a symbol of Bhutan's pristine wilderness.

The fauna of Bhutan is equally diverse and includes several endangered and rare species. The country is home to iconic animals like the Bengal Tiger, Snow Leopard, and Red Panda. Efforts to protect these species and their habitats have made Bhutan a global leader in conservation.

One of Bhutan's conservation success stories is the Takin, a unique and elusive animal sometimes referred to as the "gnarled cow of the Himalayas." It is the national animal of Bhutan and can be spotted in protected areas like Jigme Dorji National Park.

Birdwatchers flock to Bhutan for its exceptional avian diversity. The country boasts over 770 species of birds, including the endangered Black-necked Crane, which is celebrated during the annual Black-necked Crane Festival in Phobjikha Valley.

Bhutan's rivers and waterways support a variety of aquatic life, including the Golden Mahseer, a prized game fish. The country's commitment to maintaining pristine river ecosystems has helped preserve these aquatic species.

Bhutan's dedication to environmental sustainability and its emphasis on Gross National Happiness (GNH) have resulted in a strong focus on conservation. Protected areas cover more than 51% of Bhutan's total land area, ensuring that its unique flora and fauna continue to thrive.

Additionally, Bhutan's conservation efforts extend to its commitment to carbon neutrality. The country is known for its carbon-neutral status, which is achieved by maintaining forest cover, promoting renewable energy, and sustainable agricultural practices.

In conclusion, Bhutan's unique flora and fauna are a testament to the nation's dedication to preserving its natural heritage. From the lush subtropical forests to the towering Himalayan peaks, Bhutan's biodiversity is a source of pride and a reflection of the country's unwavering commitment to environmental conservation and the well-being of its people.

Conservation Efforts in Bhutan

Conservation efforts in Bhutan are a shining example of the country's unwavering commitment to preserving its pristine natural environment and the remarkable biodiversity that thrives within its borders. Nestled in the Eastern Himalayas, Bhutan has emerged as a global leader in environmental stewardship, driven by its unique development philosophy of Gross National Happiness (GNH) and a deep-rooted reverence for nature.

One of the cornerstones of Bhutan's conservation efforts is its extensive network of protected areas, covering over 51% of the country's total land area. These protected areas encompass a range of ecosystems, from dense subtropical forests in the south to alpine meadows in the north. Within these sanctuaries, rare and endangered species find refuge, including iconic creatures like the Bengal Tiger, Snow Leopard, and Red Panda.

One of the key achievements of Bhutan's conservation initiatives is the preservation of its forests. The country maintains a forest cover of over 70%, and this commitment to maintaining lush greenery has not only contributed to biodiversity conservation but also played a crucial role in mitigating climate change. Bhutan's forests act as a carbon sink, absorbing more carbon dioxide than the country emits, making it carbon-neutral. To further underscore its dedication to conservation, Bhutan has adopted innovative policies that prioritize the well-being of its citizens and the environment. The government has set strict regulations on hydropower development, ensuring that it is done sustainably and with minimal ecological impact. Additionally, Bhutan places a strong emphasis on organic farming and sustainable agriculture practices, reducing the use of harmful pesticides and chemicals. The country's commitment to conservation extends to wildlife protection. Bhutan has established several national parks, wildlife sanctuaries, and conservation areas to safeguard its unique fauna. The Black-necked Crane, an endangered bird species, finds sanctuary in the Phobjikha Valley, where an annual festival celebrates its arrival.

Another remarkable conservation effort is the Bhutan Trust Fund for Environmental Conservation (BTFEC), which provides financial support for a range of conservation projects across the country. The fund plays a pivotal role in protecting Bhutan's natural heritage and fostering community involvement in conservation activities.

Bhutan's holistic approach to conservation is closely aligned with its Gross National Happiness (GNH) philosophy, which emphasizes the importance of well-being, environmental sustainability, and cultural preservation. The GNH framework encourages balanced development that integrates economic, social, and environmental aspects, ensuring that conservation efforts benefit both people and the planet.

Tourism in Bhutan is also managed carefully to minimize its impact on the environment. The government regulates the number of tourists and enforces a daily fee that includes environmental levies, contributing to conservation efforts.

In conclusion, Bhutan's conservation efforts are a shining example of a nation's commitment to preserving its natural heritage and promoting the well-being of its citizens. With its extensive network of protected areas, sustainable policies, and a deep-rooted cultural reverence for nature, Bhutan stands as a model for responsible environmental stewardship in a rapidly changing world.

Exploring Bhutan's National Parks

Exploring Bhutan's national parks is a captivating journey into some of the world's most pristine and biodiverse landscapes. As Bhutan's commitment to environmental conservation remains unwavering, its national parks serve as protected havens for a wide array of flora and fauna, making them must-visit destinations for nature enthusiasts and adventure seekers.

One of Bhutan's iconic national parks is Jigme Dorji National Park, named after the third king of Bhutan. This expansive park, covering over 4,000 square miles, boasts a remarkable diversity of ecosystems, ranging from subtropical forests in the south to alpine meadows in the north. The park is a sanctuary for charismatic megafauna like Snow Leopards, Bengal Tigers, and Himalayan Black Bears.

Bhutan's royal heritage is reflected in the Bumdeling Wildlife Sanctuary, home to the endangered Black-necked Crane. This sanctuary, situated in the northeastern part of the country, provides a crucial wintering ground for these magnificent birds. Visitors can witness the mesmerizing sight of these cranes against the backdrop of snow-capped peaks.

To the south, Manas National Park offers a unique blend of biodiversity and cultural heritage. It's not only a UNESCO World Heritage Site but also a Biosphere Reserve. The park is a vital corridor for Asian Elephants and Indian Rhinoceroses, making it a wildlife enthusiast's paradise. It's also home to indigenous communities with their distinct cultures and traditions.

In the central region, Thrumshingla National Park beckons with its dramatic landscapes, pristine forests, and abundant birdlife. This park is a haven for birdwatchers, with over 680 bird species recorded. The elusive Satyr Tragopan and Blood Pheasant are among the avian treasures that call this park home.

For those seeking high-altitude adventure, Wangchuck Centennial Park in the north offers breathtaking vistas and a chance to explore the realm of the Himalayan Blue Sheep. This park is part of the Sacred Himalayan Landscape and is a critical conservation area for snow leopards and their prey.

While these national parks are the crown jewels of Bhutan's conservation efforts, the country's commitment to preserving its natural heritage extends to numerous other protected areas, including wildlife sanctuaries, biological corridors, and forest reserves.

Exploring Bhutan's national parks offers not only an opportunity to connect with nature but also a chance to immerse oneself in Bhutanese culture and traditions. Many of these parks are not only homes to diverse wildlife but also to monasteries, hermitages, and sacred sites that reflect the deep spiritual connection between Bhutanese people and their environment.

In conclusion, exploring Bhutan's national parks is an invitation to embark on a remarkable journey through landscapes of breathtaking beauty and ecological significance. These protected areas are a testament to Bhutan's unwavering commitment to environmental conservation and its determination to safeguard its unique natural heritage for future generations to cherish and enjoy.

The Bhutanese Approach to Sustainability

The Bhutanese approach to sustainability stands as a shining example of a nation's dedication to fostering a harmonious coexistence between its people and the environment. Rooted in the principles of Gross National Happiness (GNH), Bhutan's sustainability ethos transcends mere environmentalism; it encompasses a holistic vision of well-being, cultural preservation, and responsible governance.

At the heart of Bhutan's sustainability philosophy lies the concept of Gross National Happiness (GNH). Developed by the Fourth King of Bhutan, King Jigme Singye Wangchuck, GNH challenges the conventional notion of progress, which often equates development with economic growth alone. Instead, GNH takes into account the holistic well-being of Bhutanese citizens, considering factors such as mental and physical health, education, cultural preservation, and environmental sustainability.

One of the key pillars of Bhutanese sustainability is the country's commitment to environmental conservation. Bhutan maintains a forest cover of over 70%, which serves as a vital carbon sink and helps mitigate climate change. The government enforces strict regulations on hydropower development to ensure minimal ecological impact, and renewable energy sources are prioritized.

Bhutan's dedication to sustainability extends to agriculture. The country promotes organic farming practices, reducing the use of harmful pesticides and chemicals. This approach not only safeguards the environment but also preserves the health of its citizens and the quality of its agricultural products.

Bhutan has made significant strides in promoting gender equality and social inclusion, factors integral to sustainability. Women play active roles in Bhutanese society, including in politics, education, and the workforce. This inclusivity ensures that the benefits of development are shared equitably among all citizens.

Cultural preservation is another cornerstone of Bhutan's sustainability efforts. The country places great importance on preserving its unique heritage, including its language, traditional arts, and architecture. Bhutanese cities and towns are adorned with traditional Bhutanese architecture, featuring intricately designed buildings known as dzongs, which serve as administrative and religious centers.

Tourism in Bhutan is managed carefully to minimize its impact on the environment and culture. The government regulates the number of tourists and enforces a daily fee that includes environmental levies. This approach ensures that tourism benefits local communities and does not harm the environment.

Education is another vital component of Bhutan's sustainability strategy. The government places a strong emphasis on providing quality education to its citizens, which not only enhances human capital but also fosters a sense of social responsibility and environmental awareness.

Bhutan's commitment to sustainability is exemplified by its ambitious goals, such as becoming carbon-neutral and achieving economic self-reliance. These objectives are not mere aspirations; they are woven into the fabric of Bhutanese policy and governance.

In conclusion, the Bhutanese approach to sustainability is a multifaceted and holistic philosophy that prioritizes the well-being of its people, the preservation of its culture, and the protection of its environment. Rooted in the principles of Gross National Happiness, Bhutan's commitment to sustainability is not only a model for responsible development but also a beacon of hope in an era when environmental and societal challenges require innovative and holistic solutions.

Thimphu: The Capital City

Thimphu, the capital city of Bhutan, is a captivating blend of tradition and modernity, where the past gracefully intertwines with the present. Perched in a picturesque valley in the western part of the country, Thimphu is not only the political and administrative center of Bhutan but also a window into the nation's unique way of life.

Despite being the largest city in Bhutan, Thimphu retains a sense of charm and serenity that is characteristic of the entire country. Unlike bustling capital cities in other parts of the world, Thimphu has eschewed rapid urbanization in favor of a more measured and sustainable approach to development, in line with Bhutan's Gross National Happiness philosophy.

One of the notable features of Thimphu is its architectural aesthetics. The cityscape is dominated by traditional Bhutanese architecture, characterized by intricately designed buildings adorned with colorful paintings and woodwork. The iconic dzongs, such as the Tashichho Dzong, serve as both administrative and religious centers and are prime examples of Bhutanese architectural excellence.

Thimphu's streets are lined with prayer flags, and the melodious sound of prayer wheels being spun by devotees adds to the city's spiritual ambiance. Buddhism is an integral part of life in Thimphu, and numerous monasteries and temples dot the city, including the revered Changangkha Lhakhang.

While Thimphu embraces its traditions, it also welcomes modernity in measured doses. The city offers a glimpse of Bhutan's development journey, with well-planned roads, traffic lights, and modern infrastructure. Yet, it remains a city where you won't find a single traffic signal; instead, traffic is directed by white-gloved traffic policemen.

One of the city's most prominent landmarks is the Buddha Dordenma, a massive golden statue of Buddha that overlooks Thimphu valley. This iconic monument not only symbolizes Bhutan's Buddhist heritage but also offers panoramic views of the surrounding hills and valleys.

Thimphu is home to several cultural attractions, including the Folk Heritage Museum, which provides insights into Bhutanese rural life, and the National Textile Museum, showcasing the country's rich weaving traditions.

The city's central market, known as the Centenary Farmers' Market, is a vibrant hub where farmers from across the country converge to sell their produce. It's not just a place to buy fresh fruits and vegetables; it's a cultural experience that immerses visitors in the sights, sounds, and flavors of Bhutan.

Education and government institutions, including the National Assembly and the Royal Secretariat, are located in Thimphu. The city's educational facilities cater to students from across Bhutan, and it houses the Royal University of Bhutan.

In Thimphu, traditional customs and festivals are not forgotten. The city hosts vibrant celebrations during religious festivals like Tsechus, where masked dances, religious rituals, and cultural performances take center stage.

In conclusion, Thimphu, Bhutan's capital city, is a harmonious blend of the old and the new, where tradition is cherished, and modernity is embraced in a balanced manner. It serves a microcosm of Bhutan itself, reflecting the nation's commitment to preserving its unique heritage while moving forward on a path of responsible and sustainable development.

Paro: Gateway to Bhutan

Paro, often referred to as the "Gateway to Bhutan," is a town of profound historical and cultural significance nestled in the Paro Valley. This picturesque valley is the first point of entry for many travelers to Bhutan due to its international airport, but it's much more than just an entry point. Paro offers a rich tapestry of heritage, natural beauty, and spiritual serenity that encapsulates the essence of Bhutan.

The Paro Valley is renowned for its breathtaking landscapes, with lush green fields, terraced farms, and serene rivers meandering through the valley floor. Towering over the valley are the majestic Paro Taktsang, or Tiger's Nest Monastery, and the historic Rinpung Dzong, creating an iconic backdrop against the backdrop of the Himalayan mountains.

Paro Taktsang is perhaps Bhutan's most famous landmark, perched precariously on the edge of a cliff. The monastery holds immense spiritual significance and is associated with Guru Padmasambhava, who is said to have meditated here in the 8th century. The trek to Tiger's Nest is not just a physical journey; it's a spiritual pilgrimage that takes visitors through pristine forests and offers panoramic views of the valley below.

Rinpung Dzong, also known as the Paro Dzong, is another architectural gem in Paro. This massive fortress-monastery serves as an administrative and religious center and is a testament to Bhutanese craftsmanship and architecture. It plays a vital role in hosting the annual Paro Tsechu, a vibrant festival featuring masked dances, religious rituals, and cultural performances. The town of Paro itself is a charming blend of traditional Bhutanese architecture and modern amenities. Its streets are lined with shops selling traditional crafts, textiles, and local goods. The vibrant local market offers a glimpse into Bhutanese daily life, with farmers selling fresh produce and artisans displaying their crafts.

Paro is also home to the National Museum of Bhutan, housed in a watchtower above the Paro Dzong. The museum offers a captivating journey through Bhutan's history and culture, with an extensive collection of artifacts, art, and exhibits.

The Paro Valley is not only a place of natural beauty and cultural significance but also a region where traditional farming practices are still very much alive. The terraced fields that cover the valley are cultivated by local farmers who use age-old methods to grow crops like rice, barley, and potatoes.

The Paro International Airport, located in the valley, connects Bhutan to the world and is often considered one of the most challenging airports to land at due to its location amid the Himalayas. The flight into Paro offers breathtaking views of the mountainous terrain.

In conclusion, Paro serves as a fitting introduction to Bhutan, welcoming travelers with its natural beauty, cultural heritage, and spiritual depth. It encapsulates the essence of Bhutan, where tradition and modernity coexist harmoniously, and where every corner of the landscape holds a story of history, spirituality, and the enduring spirit of the Bhutanese people.

Punakha: The Former Capital

Punakha, often referred to as the former capital of Bhutan, holds a special place in the country's history and remains an essential part of its cultural heritage. Situated at a lower altitude than many other Bhutanese towns, Punakha enjoys a subtropical climate and is known for its lush, fertile valleys and serene rivers.

The town's significance as the former capital is tied to the Punakha Dzong, an architectural masterpiece that stands at the confluence of two major rivers, the Pho Chhu (father river) and the Mo Chhu (mother river). The dzong is an iconic symbol of Bhutanese history and culture and is often referred to as the "Palace of Great Happiness" or the "Pungthang Dewa Chenpoi Phodrang" in Bhutanese.

The construction of the Punakha Dzong dates back to the 17th century and was initiated by Zhabdrung Ngawang Namgyal, the revered leader who unified Bhutan. This majestic fortress-monastery served as the seat of Bhutan's government until the capital was moved to Thimphu in 1955. The dzong's unique architectural features, including a cantilever bridge, beautiful murals, and intricate woodwork, make it one of the most photogenic and historically significant structures in Bhutan.

Punakha is also associated with important events in Bhutanese royal history. The wedding of the beloved King Jigme Khesar Namgyel Wangchuck and Queen Jetsun Pema took place in Punakha Dzong in 2011, attracting attention and well-wishes from around the world.

Aside from its historical significance, Punakha boasts natural beauty that complements its cultural treasures. The valley is characterized by emerald-green terraced fields of rice and a climate that supports the cultivation of oranges, bananas, and other subtropical fruits. The Mo Chhu and Pho Chhu rivers add to the town's charm, offering opportunities for activities like white-water rafting and leisurely walks along their banks.

Punakha's tranquil ambiance and mild climate make it an ideal destination for travelers looking to explore Bhutan's cultural heritage and natural beauty. The town's proximity to the capital, Thimphu, and other significant regions in Bhutan make it a convenient stop for those traversing the country.

In conclusion, Punakha, as the former capital of Bhutan, holds a unique place in the nation's history and culture. Its iconic Punakha Dzong, set against the backdrop of lush valleys and rivers, serves as a testament to Bhutan's rich heritage. Whether for its historical significance or its natural beauty, Punakha continues to captivate and inspire visitors, offering a glimpse into the heart of Bhutan.

The Historic City of Bumthang

The historic city of Bumthang, nestled in the central part of Bhutan, is a cultural and spiritual treasure trove that beckons travelers seeking a deeper connection with Bhutan's rich heritage. Comprising four distinct valleys - Chokhor, Tang, Ura, and Chhume - Bumthang is often referred to as the "Switzerland of Bhutan" due to its alpine scenery and lush forests.

At the heart of Bumthang lies Jakar, the main town and administrative center of the region. Jakar is characterized by its quaint charm, with traditional Bhutanese architecture, prayer flags fluttering in the breeze, and fertile fields surrounding the town. The Jakar Dzong, also known as the "Castle of the White Bird," is a prominent feature, overseeing the town from a hilltop.

Bumthang is steeped in history and mythology. Legend has it that the valley is the resting place of the great Tibetan saint Guru Padmasambhava, who is said to have subdued local demons and introduced Buddhism to the region in the 8th century. Many of the temples and monasteries in Bumthang are associated with Guru Rinpoche, making it a sacred pilgrimage site for Buddhists.

One of the most revered religious sites in Bumthang is the Kurjey Lhakhang, named after a body print of Guru Padmasambhava that is preserved here. The temple complex also includes three other temples, each with its own historical and spiritual significance.

Another significant religious site is the Jambay Lhakhang, one of Bhutan's oldest temples, believed to have been built by King Songtsen Gampo of Tibet in the 7th century. The temple hosts the famous Jambay Lhakhang Drup festival, featuring traditional masked dances and rituals.

Bumthang is also known for its natural beauty, with pristine forests, meandering rivers, and serene lakes. The Tang Valley, in particular, offers enchanting landscapes and the opportunity for treks and nature walks. The Ura Valley, on the other hand, is known for its picturesque landscape, traditional architecture, and the Ura Yakchoe festival.

The people of Bumthang are warm and welcoming, and the region's unique culture and traditions are well-preserved. Visitors have the chance to experience traditional Bhutanese hospitality and may even be invited into local homes to sample traditional dishes.

In conclusion, the historic city of Bumthang is a captivating destination that offers a deep dive into Bhutan's spiritual and cultural heritage. With its sacred sites, lush landscapes, and rich history, Bumthang beckons travelers to explore its serene valleys and immerse themselves in the timeless traditions that define this remarkable region of Bhutan.

Glimpses of Rural Life in Bhutan

Glimpses of rural life in Bhutan offer a profound and authentic understanding of the nation's culture, traditions, and the enduring connection between its people and the land they inhabit. Bhutan's rural landscape is a tapestry of terraced fields, traditional farmhouses, and pristine natural beauty, providing a stark contrast to the bustling urban centers.

In Bhutan's rural communities, agriculture is the backbone of daily life. Families cultivate their land using age-old techniques, tilling the earth with oxen or yaks and planting crops like rice, barley, and potatoes. The rhythm of life here follows the seasons, with sowing and harvesting times marked by festivals and rituals that celebrate the agricultural cycle.

Traditional farmhouses, with their distinctive Bhutanese architecture, are scattered across the countryside. These two-story wooden structures house both families and their livestock, a reflection of the close bond between humans and animals in rural Bhutan. The ground floor serves as a shelter for cattle, while the upper floor is the living area for the family.

Rural Bhutanese are known for their strong sense of community. Villages come together for various activities, from building houses and bridges to planting and harvesting crops. Such communal labor, known as "zhogde," embodies the spirit of cooperation that has sustained these communities for generations. One of the most remarkable aspects of rural life in Bhutan is the preservation of traditional customs and culture. People in these communities wear their distinctive traditional attire daily, proudly displaying their cultural identity. The Gho for men and Kira for women are not just clothing but a reflection of Bhutanese identity and heritage.

Villages often have a central temple or monastery, where Buddhist monks play an integral role in the spiritual life of the community. Monastic festivals, or Tsechus, are celebrated with great fervor in rural areas, featuring colorful mask dances, religious rituals, and a sense of shared spirituality.

In rural Bhutan, the concept of Gross National Happiness (GNH) isn't an abstract idea but a lived experience. The close-knit communities, connection to the land, and adherence to cultural traditions contribute to the well-being and contentment of the people. The peaceful surroundings, away from the hustle and bustle of urban life, provide a sense of tranquility that is intrinsic to Bhutanese rural life.

Despite the modernization efforts in Bhutan, many rural areas remain untouched by the fast pace of change. However, the government is working to ensure that rural communities have access to education, healthcare, and other essential services while preserving their unique way of life.

In conclusion, glimpses of rural life in Bhutan reveal a world where tradition, community, and a deep connection to the land continue to shape the daily existence of its people. It is a testament to Bhutan's commitment to Gross National Happiness, where the well-being of its citizens is intricately woven into the fabric of its rural communities, ensuring a harmonious balance between tradition and progress.

Exploring the Eastern Bhutan Region

Exploring the Eastern Bhutan region is a journey into the less-trodden paths of this enigmatic Himalayan nation. While Western Bhutan has garnered much attention for its iconic attractions, the east remains a hidden gem waiting to be discovered. This remote and less-visited part of Bhutan offers a unique blend of natural beauty, cultural richness, and traditional way of life.

The eastern region of Bhutan encompasses several districts, including Trashigang, Mongar, Lhuentse, and Tashiyangtse. It is known for its rugged terrain, deep valleys, and dense forests. The region's topography is dominated by steep hills and winding rivers, creating a landscape that is both challenging and captivating for adventurers.

One of the highlights of the Eastern Bhutan region is the stunning Trashigang Dzong, perched on a hilltop overlooking the Gamri River. This imposing fortress-monastery is not only an architectural marvel but also an important administrative center for the district. Its location offers breathtaking views of the surrounding valleys and mountains.

The eastern region is known for its rich textile traditions, with Lhuentse district being famous for producing some of the finest handwoven textiles in Bhutan. The intricate patterns and vibrant colors of Lhuentse textiles are a testament to the skill and dedication of local weavers.

Exploring the remote villages of Eastern Bhutan provides a glimpse into the traditional way of life of its people. Farming is the primary occupation, and rice, maize, and millet are the staple crops. Villagers live in charming traditional Bhutanese houses, often adorned with intricate woodwork and paintings.

Bhutan's eastern region is also home to several wildlife sanctuaries and parks, including the Bumdeling Wildlife Sanctuary and the Khaling Wildlife Sanctuary. These protected areas provide habitat for diverse species of flora and fauna, including the elusive snow leopard and red panda.

Trekking and hiking enthusiasts will find Eastern Bhutan to be a paradise for outdoor adventures. The Merak-Sakteng trek, for example, takes you through remote highland villages, offering a unique cultural experience along with stunning vistas of the eastern Himalayas.

The region is also known for its vibrant festivals, such as the Mongar Tshechu and the Trashigang Tshechu. These festivals showcase traditional Bhutanese dance, music, and religious rituals, providing an opportunity to immerse in the local culture.

Eastern Bhutan's remoteness has allowed it to preserve its authenticity and cultural heritage. While it may require more effort to reach this part of the country, the rewards are in the form of untouched landscapes, encounters with friendly locals, and a sense of stepping back in time to experience Bhutan as it once was.

In conclusion, exploring the Eastern Bhutan region is an adventure into a lesser-known, yet equally captivating, side of this Himalayan kingdom. It offers a chance to connect with nature, appreciate Bhutanese traditions, and witness a way of life that remains deeply rooted in tradition and untouched by the rapid pace of modernization.

Bhutan's Remote Villages and Valleys

Bhutan's remote villages and valleys are like hidden treasures tucked away in the folds of the Himalayas. These isolated communities offer a glimpse into a way of life that has remained largely untouched by the modern world, where tradition, culture, and a deep connection to the land define daily existence.

One such remote valley is Phobjikha, located in the heart of Bhutan. This pristine valley is renowned for its stunning natural beauty and is often called the "Valley of the Black-Necked Cranes." Each winter, these graceful birds migrate to Phobjikha from Tibet, creating a mesmerizing spectacle against the backdrop of the Gangteng Monastery.

Another remote gem is the Haa Valley, situated in the western part of Bhutan. It was opened to tourists only in 2002, preserving its pristine landscapes and traditional way of life. The valley is dotted with charming villages, and the Haa Summer Festival showcases the rich cultural heritage of the region.

The remote village of Merak and Sakteng, located in the eastern part of Bhutan, offers a truly off-the-beaten-path experience. These highland villages are inhabited by the semi-nomadic Brokpa people, known for their unique culture, clothing, and traditions. Trekking to Merak and Sakteng is an adventure into a world where time seems to have stood still.

In the far east of Bhutan, you'll find the remote and rugged Lunana region. It's one of the most isolated parts of the country and home to the Snowman Trek, one of the world's most challenging trekking routes. The people of Lunana, known as the Layaps, lead a life that revolves around yak herding and farming, and their way of life is a testament to resilience in the face of harsh conditions.

The villages and valleys of Bhutan's remote regions are often accessible only by winding mountain roads or treacherous trails, adding to their sense of isolation. Yet, these regions are not just about physical remoteness but also about preserving Bhutan's cultural and natural heritage.

In these remote communities, traditional architecture is still prevalent, with houses made of mud and stone, often adorned with intricate woodwork. The people here rely on subsistence farming, growing crops like buckwheat, maize, and potatoes on terraced fields that have been cultivated for centuries.

The isolation of these villages has led to the preservation of traditional Bhutanese customs and clothing. The Gho and Kira, Bhutan's national dress, are worn with pride, and festivals and religious rituals are celebrated with deep devotion.

These remote regions are also vital for biodiversity conservation. Bhutan's government recognizes the importance of protecting these pristine landscapes and has designated many of them as national parks and wildlife sanctuaries.

In conclusion, Bhutan's remote villages and valleys are pockets of authenticity and natural beauty in an increasingly interconnected world. They offer a unique opportunity to witness a way of life that is deeply rooted in tradition, where the land, culture, and spirituality are intertwined. Exploring these remote corners of Bhutan is not just a physical journey but a voyage into the heart and soul of this extraordinary nation.

The Iconic Tiger's Nest Monastery

The iconic Tiger's Nest Monastery, also known as Paro Taktsang, is perhaps the most famous and recognizable symbol of Bhutan. Perched dramatically on the edge of a sheer cliff, this sacred site is not only a marvel of architectural and engineering ingenuity but also a testament to the profound spirituality that permeates Bhutanese culture.

Nestled in the Paro Valley, the Tiger's Nest Monastery is a place of pilgrimage and reverence for Buddhists and a source of wonder for travelers from around the world. The legend surrounding its origins is both mystical and inspiring. It is said that Guru Padmasambhava, the revered Indian saint who brought Buddhism to Bhutan, flew to this location on the back of a tigress in the 8th century.

The trek to Tiger's Nest is an adventure in itself, taking you through a lush forest of blue pine trees and rhododendrons. As you ascend the steep path, the views become increasingly breathtaking. The monastery seems to defy gravity as it clings to the cliffside, a sight that leaves an indelible impression on all who visit.

The complex comprises several temples and buildings, all interconnected by narrow staircases and winding pathways. Each structure is a masterpiece of Bhutanese architecture, adorned with colorful frescoes, intricate woodwork, and sacred relics. The main temple houses a statue of Guru Padmasambhava, where pilgrims come to offer prayers and seek blessings.

Visiting Tiger's Nest is not just a physical journey but also a spiritual one. The serene ambiance, the sound of prayer flags fluttering in the wind, and the sight of devotees lighting butter lamps create an atmosphere of deep reverence and contemplation.

The monastery also plays a crucial role in Bhutanese culture and history. It was here that Guru Padmasambhava is believed to have meditated for three years, three months, three weeks, and three days, subduing local demons and imparting profound teachings. His spiritual legacy lives on in the hearts of Bhutanese people, and Tiger's Nest stands as a symbol of his enlightenment.

The preservation of this sacred site is of paramount importance to Bhutan's government, and efforts are made to ensure its structural integrity and protection from natural disasters. Restoration work is carried out with great care to maintain the authenticity of the monastery.

In conclusion, the Tiger's Nest Monastery is not merely a physical structure but a spiritual beacon that draws both pilgrims and travelers into its mystical embrace. Its precarious perch on a cliff, its rich history, and its enduring spiritual significance make it a symbol of Bhutan's cultural and religious heritage. Visiting Tiger's Nest is a transformative experience, leaving an indelible mark on those who make the journey to this iconic Bhutanese treasure.

Other Must-Visit Monasteries and Temples

Bhutan is a land of monasteries and temples, each with its own unique charm, history, and spiritual significance. While the Tiger's Nest Monastery is the most famous, there are many other must-visit religious sites that offer a deeper understanding of Bhutanese culture and Buddhism.

1. Punakha Dzong: This majestic fortress-monastery is not only one of Bhutan's most beautiful structures but also a historical and spiritual hub. Located at the confluence of the Pho Chhu and Mo Chhu rivers, Punakha Dzong served as the winter capital of Bhutan until the 1950s. The annual Punakha Tshechu, a vibrant religious festival, is held here.

2. Kyichu Lhakhang: This ancient temple in Paro is one of Bhutan's oldest and holiest shrines. It was built in the 7th century by King Songtsen Gampo of Tibet, and it houses sacred relics and intricate murals. The temple is renowned for its two orange trees, said to bear fruit throughout the year.

3. Gangtey Monastery: Also known as Gangtey Goenpa, this serene monastery sits in the Phobjikha Valley, one of the most beautiful glacial valleys in Bhutan. It is a center for Nyingma Buddhism and offers stunning views of the valley and its resident black-necked cranes.

4. Rinpung Dzong: Located in Paro, Rinpung Dzong is a fortress-monastery that overlooks the Paro Valley. It is famous for its massive white walls, beautiful paintings, and the Paro Tsechu festival. The dzong also houses administrative offices.

5. Chimi Lhakhang: This unique temple, also known as the "Temple of the Divine Madman," is dedicated to Drukpa Kunley, a Buddhist saint known for his eccentric behavior. It is a pilgrimage site for couples seeking blessings for fertility and protection from evil spirits.

6. Tashichho Dzong: Situated in Thimphu, the capital of Bhutan, Tashichho Dzong is both an administrative and religious center. It houses the throne room of the King of Bhutan, the main secretariat, and several government offices. The annual Thimphu Tshechu is celebrated here.

7. Lhodrak Kharchhu Monastery: Nestled in the hills above the Haa Valley, this monastery is renowned for its beautiful location and as the residence of the late Dilgo Khyentse Rinpoche, a revered Tibetan Buddhist master.

8. Kurjey Lhakhang: Located in Bumthang, Kurjey Lhakhang is famous for its three temples, with the oldest dating back to the 8th century. It holds a body print of Guru Padmasambhava, making it a significant pilgrimage site.

9. Jambay Lhakhang: Another important temple in Bumthang, Jambay Lhakhang is believed to have been constructed by King Songtsen Gampo of Tibet in the 7th century. The Jambay Lhakhang Drup festival is a major event here.

10. Kila Goenpa: Perched high on a cliff, this monastery offers a challenging hike and breathtaking views of the Paro Valley. It is a place of meditation and retreat for monks.

These are just a few of the many monasteries and temples that dot the Bhutanese landscape. Each holds its own significance in the spiritual and cultural tapestry of Bhutan, offering visitors a chance to delve deeper into the nation's rich heritage and traditions.

Bhutan's Trekking and Hiking Trails

Bhutan's trekking and hiking trails are a dream come true for outdoor enthusiasts and adventure seekers. The rugged terrain of this Himalayan kingdom offers a variety of trekking experiences, from challenging high-altitude journeys to more leisurely hikes through pristine forests and remote villages. Here, the mountains are not just a backdrop; they are the main attraction.

The Snowman Trek, often considered one of the world's toughest treks, traverses high mountain passes, remote valleys, and offers a glimpse into the lives of nomadic yak herders. This epic journey spans about 220 miles and crosses 11 passes over 13,000 feet, taking trekkers through some of Bhutan's most remote and breathtaking landscapes.

For those seeking a shorter but equally spectacular trek, the Jomolhari Trek is a popular choice. This trail takes you to the base of Bhutan's sacred mountain, Jomolhari, where you can enjoy panoramic views of the snow-capped peaks.

The Druk Path Trek is another favorite, known for its moderate difficulty level and the opportunity to visit some of Bhutan's iconic monasteries, such as the Tango and Cheri Monasteries near Thimphu.

If you're looking for a cultural trek, the Laya-Gasa Trek allows you to immerse yourself in the unique culture of the Layap people while trekking through lush forests and high passes. Bhutan's eastern region offers the Merak-Sakteng Trek, which takes you to the remote villages of Merak and

Sakteng, inhabited by the Brokpa people. This trek combines cultural experiences with stunning landscapes.

The Bumthang Owl Trek is ideal for those interested in exploring Bhutan's heartland and visiting its historic temples and monasteries. It's a relatively gentle trek suitable for most fitness levels.

In the Phobjikha Valley, you can take the Gangtey Trek, which offers the chance to see the rare black-necked cranes during their winter migration. The trek takes you through beautiful meadows and forests.

While these are just a few examples, Bhutan offers a multitude of trekking and hiking opportunities, each with its own unique appeal. The trails pass through lush valleys, dense forests, alpine meadows, and remote villages, providing a chance to connect with nature and the local way of life.

Bhutan's government places a strong emphasis on sustainable tourism, ensuring that these pristine landscapes are preserved for generations to come. Trekkers are encouraged to follow Leave No Trace principles and respect the natural environment.

In conclusion, Bhutan's trekking and hiking trails are a gateway to adventure, natural beauty, and cultural immersion. Whether you're an experienced trekker seeking a challenging high-altitude expedition or a casual hiker looking for a leisurely stroll through picturesque landscapes, Bhutan has a trail to match your interests and abilities, making it a trekker's paradise in the heart of the Himalayas.

Adventure Activities in Bhutan

Bhutan is not just a destination for cultural exploration and trekking; it's also an adventure enthusiast's playground. The rugged terrain, pristine rivers, and lush forests provide the perfect backdrop for a wide range of adrenaline-pumping activities. Here, you can combine your love for adventure with the awe-inspiring beauty of the Himalayas.

1. **White-Water Rafting:** Bhutan's rivers, including the Paro Chhu, Mo Chhu, and Pho Chhu, offer thrilling white-water rafting opportunities. The rapids vary in intensity, making it suitable for both beginners and experienced rafters. Rafting through deep gorges and pristine wilderness is an exhilarating way to experience Bhutan's natural beauty.
2. **Kayaking:** For those who prefer a more intimate experience with the water, kayaking is a fantastic option. Bhutan's rivers provide excellent conditions for kayaking, with opportunities for both beginners and experts. The Mo Chhu and Pho Chhu rivers are popular kayaking spots.
3. **Mountain Biking:** Bhutan's winding mountain roads and off-road trails are a haven for mountain biking enthusiasts. You can explore the countryside, visit remote villages, and enjoy breathtaking views of the Himalayas while pedaling through this scenic landscape.
4. **Rock Climbing:** The cliffs and rock formations in Bhutan offer exciting rock climbing experiences. Climbing enthusiasts can enjoy both traditional

climbing and bouldering in various locations, including the Paro Valley and Thimphu.

5. **Trekking and Hiking:** While trekking was mentioned earlier, it's worth emphasizing that Bhutan offers a wide range of trekking options, from challenging high-altitude treks to shorter, more leisurely hikes. The variety of landscapes and trails means there's a trek suitable for every level of fitness and experience.

6. **Cycling:** Beyond mountain biking, cycling is a great way to explore Bhutan's countryside and interact with locals. You can cycle through picturesque valleys, visit monasteries, and take in the scenic beauty of the country.

7. **Fishing:** Bhutan's rivers are teeming with trout, making it an excellent destination for fishing enthusiasts. You can try your hand at fly fishing in the clear mountain streams while enjoying the tranquility of nature.

8. **Archery:** While archery is not typically associated with extreme adventure, it's Bhutan's national sport and can be a thrilling experience for visitors. You can participate in archery competitions and immerse yourself in this unique cultural activity.

9. **Paragliding:** Paragliding in Bhutan offers a bird's-eye view of the stunning landscapes below. Soaring above lush valleys and monasteries is an experience you won't soon forget.

10. **Wildlife Safaris:** Bhutan is home to a rich variety of wildlife, including Bengal tigers, snow leopards, and red pandas. Wildlife safaris and treks provide the opportunity to spot these elusive creatures in their natural habitats.

11. **Hot Air Ballooning:** For a more serene adventure, you can take a hot air balloon ride over Bhutan's

valleys and monasteries. It's a unique way to appreciate the country's diverse landscapes.

Adventure activities in Bhutan are not just about seeking thrills; they also offer a deeper connection with the country's natural beauty and cultural heritage. Whether you're navigating white-water rapids, pedaling through picturesque villages, or soaring through the sky, Bhutan's adventures are sure to leave you with lasting memories of this extraordinary Himalayan kingdom.

Bhutan's Traditional Medicine: Sowa Rigpa

Bhutan's traditional medicine system, known as Sowa Rigpa, has deep roots in the country's culture and history. It is an ancient healing tradition that has been passed down through generations, offering a holistic approach to health and well-being. Sowa Rigpa is not only a medical system but also a way of life, reflecting Bhutan's commitment to preserving its rich heritage.

Sowa Rigpa translates to the "Science of Healing" and encompasses various aspects of traditional medicine, including herbal medicine, diet, lifestyle, and spiritual practices. It is influenced by Buddhist principles and the belief that harmony between the body and mind is essential for good health.

Key Components of Sowa Rigpa:

1. **Herbal Medicine:** At the heart of Sowa Rigpa is the use of medicinal plants. Bhutan boasts a rich biodiversity, and traditional healers have a profound knowledge of the healing properties of indigenous herbs. These herbal remedies are often prepared following precise recipes passed down through generations.
2. **Diet and Nutrition:** Sowa Rigpa emphasizes the importance of a balanced diet tailored to an individual's constitution and health condition. Dietary guidelines are derived from traditional knowledge and are adjusted seasonally.

3. **Lifestyle and Behavior:** The traditional medicine system takes into account the impact of lifestyle choices on health. It encourages practices such as meditation, yoga, and specific exercises to promote physical and mental well-being.
4. **Diagnosis:** Traditional practitioners in Bhutan use a combination of techniques for diagnosis, including pulse reading, urine analysis, and visual examination of the tongue, nails, and eyes. These methods help identify imbalances in the body's energies.
5. **Treatment:** Treatment in Sowa Rigpa aims to restore the balance of the body's three main energies: Wind (Lung), Bile (Tripa), and Phlegm (Pekan). Depending on the diagnosis, treatments may include herbal remedies, dietary changes, external therapies like massages, and lifestyle recommendations.
6. **Spiritual and Mental Well-being:** Sowa Rigpa acknowledges the intimate connection between the mind and the body. Practices such as meditation and mindfulness are incorporated into the healing process to address mental and emotional aspects of health.
7. **Training and Certification:** Bhutan has established formal institutions for the study and practice of Sowa Rigpa. Traditional medicine practitioners undergo rigorous training and must meet certification standards to ensure the quality of care.

Sowa Rigpa plays a vital role in Bhutan's healthcare system, running in parallel with modern Western medicine. Patients have the choice to seek treatment from either system or even combine them. The Bhutanese government recognizes the value of traditional medicine and has established the Menjong Sorig Pharmaceuticals Corporation to produce traditional medicines and promote their use.

Furthermore, Bhutan's commitment to preserving its cultural heritage includes the conservation and documentation of traditional medicinal knowledge. Efforts are made to safeguard the country's diverse flora and the indigenous knowledge associated with it.

In conclusion, Bhutan's traditional medicine system, Sowa Rigpa, embodies the country's deep-rooted cultural and spiritual values. It not only provides healthcare solutions but also fosters a profound connection between individuals and the natural world. Sowa Rigpa is a testament to Bhutan's commitment to holistic well-being and the preservation of its unique heritage.

Bhutan's Unique Postal Service

Bhutan's postal service is unlike any other in the world. It's a charming and distinctive aspect of this small Himalayan kingdom that captures the essence of Bhutanese culture and the nation's commitment to preserving its heritage in a rapidly modernizing world.

History of Bhutan's Postal Service:

The Bhutanese postal system has a rich history dating back to the early 17th century when Zhabdrung Ngawang Namgyal, the unifier of Bhutan, established a network of postal runners to carry messages between dzongs (fortresses) and important centers. These runners, known as "lamas," were often monks who could traverse the rugged terrain, ensuring communication even in the most remote areas.

The Iconic Postal Runners:

The image of Bhutan's postal runners, dressed in traditional gho (men's robe) and carrying bamboo containers strapped to their backs, has become iconic. These runners, who cover long distances on foot, remain an integral part of Bhutan's postal service, blending tradition and modernity.

Bhutan's Unique Postage Stamps:

One of the standout features of Bhutan's postal service is its innovative approach to postage stamps. Bhutan is renowned for issuing stamps that are not just functional but also highly collectible. In the 1970s, Bhutan gained international attention for releasing postage stamps in unconventional shapes, including ones shaped like fruits, animals, and even record discs. These creative stamps sparked global interest and are prized by philatelists worldwide.

Philately and the Postal Museum:

Bhutan's passion for stamps and postal history is evident in its Postal Museum in Thimphu, which showcases the evolution of Bhutan's postal system and its unique postage stamps. Visitors can explore the history of Bhutanese communication, view rare stamps, and gain insight into the country's cultural heritage.

Traditional Mail Delivery:

Even today, in the age of digital communication, Bhutan's postal service continues to provide an essential means of communication, particularly in remote regions where modern infrastructure is limited. Letters and parcels are often delivered by hand, ensuring that messages reach even the most isolated communities.

The Future of Bhutan's Postal Service:

While Bhutan's postal service retains its traditional charm, it has also adapted to the digital age. Bhutan Post, the country's postal authority, offers services like express mail, e-commerce solutions, and money transfer services, ensuring that it remains relevant in the 21st century.

The Bhutanese Post Office Network:

The Bhutan Post has an extensive network of post offices and access points across the country, including in rural areas. This ensures that Bhutanese citizens, regardless of their location, have access to postal services.

In conclusion, Bhutan's postal service is a unique blend of tradition and innovation. It combines the timeless image of postal runners in traditional attire with a commitment to providing modern postal solutions to its citizens. Bhutan's creative postage stamps, its iconic postal runners, and the preservation of its postal heritage make it a noteworthy aspect of this enchanting Himalayan kingdom.

Bhutan's Approach to Environmental Conservation

Bhutan's approach to environmental conservation is nothing short of inspirational. It's a country that takes its commitment to preserving its natural heritage seriously, and this dedication is woven into the very fabric of Bhutanese society and government policies.

The Birth of Gross National Happiness:

Bhutan is famous for its unique philosophy of Gross National Happiness (GNH), which prioritizes the well-being and happiness of its citizens over economic growth alone. This holistic approach to development encompasses environmental sustainability as a core pillar. Bhutan recognizes that a healthy environment is intrinsically linked to the well-being of its people.

Carbon-Neutral Bhutan:

One of Bhutan's most remarkable environmental achievements is its status as a carbon-neutral nation. This means that Bhutan's carbon emissions are offset by the carbon sequestration of its forests. The country's lush forests act as carbon sinks, absorbing more carbon dioxide than the nation emits. It's a remarkable feat that demonstrates Bhutan's commitment to combatting climate change.

Conservation of Biodiversity:

Bhutan's breathtaking landscapes, from dense forests to towering peaks, are home to a diverse array of wildlife. The country has set aside a significant portion of its land as protected areas and national parks to safeguard this rich biodiversity. The royal government of Bhutan has implemented strict conservation measures to protect endangered species such as the Bengal tiger and snow leopard.

Hydropower and Sustainable Energy:

Bhutan is also a leader in renewable energy. It harnesses the power of its rivers for hydropower generation, providing clean energy not only for its own citizens but also exporting surplus electricity to neighboring countries. This sustainable approach to energy production reduces reliance on fossil fuels and promotes environmental sustainability.

Sustainable Agriculture:

In Bhutan, traditional farming practices are still prevalent, with an emphasis on organic and sustainable agriculture. The use of chemical pesticides and fertilizers is discouraged, and the country strives to maintain its status as an organic farming nation. This approach not only ensures food security but also protects the environment from harmful agricultural practices.

Preservation of Cultural Landscapes:

Bhutan's cultural heritage is closely tied to its natural landscapes. The country places great importance on preserving its cultural heritage, including the intricate architecture of dzongs (fortresses) and monasteries. This preservation extends to the surrounding natural environments, ensuring that both cultural and natural heritage are safeguarded.

Environmental Education and Awareness:

Bhutan recognizes the importance of educating its citizens about environmental conservation. Environmental education is integrated into the school curriculum, and public awareness campaigns promote responsible environmental practices.

Global Environmental Leadership:

Despite its small size, Bhutan plays a significant role on the global stage in advocating for environmental conservation and sustainable development. The country actively participates in international forums and initiatives related to climate change and biodiversity conservation.

In conclusion, Bhutan's approach to environmental conservation is a shining example of how a nation can prioritize the well-being of its people and the preservation of its natural heritage. The kingdom's commitment to Gross National Happiness, carbon neutrality, biodiversity conservation, sustainable energy, and cultural preservation sets it apart as a global leader in environmental sustainability. Bhutan's story serves as an inspiration for the world, showing that a harmonious relationship between humans and nature is not only possible but essential for a thriving future.

Bhutan's Foreign Relations and Diplomacy

Bhutan's foreign relations and diplomacy are characterized by a careful and deliberate approach that seeks to protect the nation's sovereignty, promote its unique cultural identity, and ensure its economic well-being. This landlocked Himalayan kingdom, nestled between two giants, India and China, has pursued a policy of strategic balancing while maintaining friendly ties with its neighbors and engaging constructively with the international community.

The India-Bhutan Friendship Treaty:

At the core of Bhutan's foreign relations is the India-Bhutan Friendship Treaty, signed in 1949. This treaty has been crucial in shaping Bhutan's diplomatic stance. It outlines India's responsibility for Bhutan's defense and allows Bhutan to conduct its foreign affairs under the guidance of India. This treaty has provided Bhutan with security and economic assistance and has been the cornerstone of its foreign policy.

China: Balancing Act in the Dragon's Shadow:

Bhutan shares a disputed border with China, which has occasionally led to tensions, most notably in the Doklam standoff in 2017. Bhutan has maintained a cautious and diplomatic approach to its relationship with China, focusing on boundary negotiations while striving to ensure its sovereignty is respected.

Nonalignment and Peaceful Coexistence:

Bhutan adheres to a policy of nonalignment, which means it avoids taking sides in international conflicts and maintains peaceful coexistence with all nations. This neutrality has allowed Bhutan to engage in international diplomacy without becoming entangled in geopolitical rivalries.

International Organizations:

Bhutan is a member of several international organizations, including the United Nations, where it actively participates in discussions on global issues such as climate change, sustainable development, and disarmament. The country's commitment to Gross National Happiness has also influenced its engagement with international organizations, advocating for well-being as a key metric of global progress.

Economic Diplomacy:

Bhutan has actively pursued economic diplomacy to enhance its economic well-being. It has engaged in trade agreements with neighboring countries, particularly India, to promote the export of hydroelectric power and other goods. This economic cooperation has been instrumental in Bhutan's development.

Cultural Diplomacy:

Bhutan's unique culture and heritage play a significant role in its diplomatic endeavors. The country has focused on cultural exchanges and tourism promotion to strengthen people-to-people ties with other nations. The concept of "high-value, low-impact" tourism has been embraced to preserve Bhutan's pristine environment and culture.

Humanitarian Engagement:

Bhutan has contributed to humanitarian efforts by participating in international peacekeeping missions and providing humanitarian assistance in times of crisis. Its commitment to GNH has also inspired discussions on well-being and happiness at the global level.

In conclusion, Bhutan's foreign relations and diplomacy reflect its commitment to preserving its sovereignty, promoting its cultural identity, and securing its economic well-being. Through a careful and strategic approach, Bhutan has maintained friendly ties with its neighbors, engaged with the international community, and actively participated in global discussions on pressing issues. Despite its small size, Bhutan's diplomatic efforts have positioned it as a respected and influential player on the world stage.

Bhutan's Role in the South Asian Region

Bhutan's role in the South Asian region is both unique and significant. Despite its small size and relatively isolated location in the Himalayas, Bhutan has played a noteworthy role in regional affairs, contributing to the stability and development of South Asia. Here, we explore Bhutan's diplomatic engagements, regional partnerships, and its impact on the South Asian region.

The Stabilizing Force of Bhutan:

Bhutan is often referred to as the "Land of the Thunder Dragon," and its role in the South Asian region is akin to that of a calm and stabilizing force amidst the sometimes turbulent geopolitics of South Asia. Its commitment to maintaining peaceful relations with its neighbors, particularly India and China, has contributed to regional stability.

The India-Bhutan Friendship Treaty:

Central to Bhutan's regional engagement is its relationship with India. The India-Bhutan Friendship Treaty of 1949 has not only ensured Bhutan's security but has also made India a crucial partner in Bhutan's development. India has supported Bhutan in various sectors, including infrastructure, education, and hydropower, contributing to Bhutan's economic growth.

China's Growing Influence:

Bhutan's proximity to China has also influenced its regional role. The dispute over the Doklam plateau in 2017 brought Bhutan into the spotlight as it sought to protect its territory and sovereignty. Bhutan has maintained a delicate balancing act in its relations with both India and China, ensuring its interests are safeguarded.

Regional Organizations:

Bhutan is a member of the South Asian Association for Regional Cooperation (SAARC), a regional organization that fosters cooperation and development among South Asian nations. While Bhutan's participation in SAARC has been active, regional dynamics have sometimes influenced its level of engagement.

Hydropower and Regional Energy Cooperation:

Bhutan's abundant water resources have positioned it as a potential energy hub in the region. It has been actively engaged in exporting hydroelectric power to India, contributing to India's energy needs. This cooperation has strengthened the economic ties between the two nations.

Contributions to Regional Peacekeeping:

Despite its small military, Bhutan has made contributions to regional peacekeeping efforts. It has sent troops to participate in United Nations peacekeeping missions, demonstrating its commitment to global and regional security.

Environmental Leadership:

Bhutan's dedication to environmental conservation and sustainable development has resonated in the South Asian region. It has advocated for climate action and sustainability in regional forums, emphasizing the importance of preserving the Himalayan ecosystem.

In conclusion, Bhutan's role in the South Asian region is characterized by its commitment to peace, stability, and sustainable development. Despite its size, Bhutan has been an influential player in regional affairs, maintaining strong partnerships with neighboring countries while navigating complex geopolitical dynamics. Its unique position in the Himalayas and its dedication to Gross National Happiness have made it a respected and valued member of the South Asian community, contributing to the region's well-being and prosperity.

Bhutanese Folklore and Myths

Bhutanese folklore and myths are a treasure trove of stories that have been passed down through generations, shaping the cultural identity of the Bhutanese people. These tales are not just entertaining narratives; they are windows into the beliefs, values, and traditions that define Bhutanese society. Let's delve into the rich tapestry of Bhutanese folklore and myths.

Origin Myths:

Bhutan, like many cultures, has its own origin myths that explain the creation of the land and its people. These myths often involve celestial beings, deities, and legendary figures. They provide a sense of connection between the Bhutanese people and the land they inhabit.

Deities and Guardians:

Bhutanese folklore is replete with stories of deities and guardian spirits. These supernatural beings are believed to watch over the people and the land, offering protection and guidance. Local temples and shrines often pay homage to these deities, and rituals are performed to honor them.

The Yeti - The Elusive Snowman:

Bhutan is home to the mysterious creature known as the Yeti, or the "Migoi" in Bhutanese folklore. These tales of encounters with the elusive snowman have fueled the imaginations of both locals and adventurers from around the world. The Yeti remains an enduring legend in Bhutanese culture.

Folk Heroes and Epic Tales:

Bhutan has its own folk heroes and epic tales that celebrate bravery, resourcefulness, and heroism. One of the most famous is the story of Pema Lingpa, a renowned Bhutanese treasure revealer and saint. His legendary feats and teachings continue to inspire Bhutanese people.

Talking Animals and Magical Objects:

Bhutanese folklore often features talking animals, magical objects, and enchanted landscapes. These elements add whimsy and wonder to the stories and are a testament to the imaginative storytelling tradition of Bhutan.

Moral Lessons and Values:

Many Bhutanese folktales convey important moral lessons and values, teaching virtues such as kindness, honesty, and humility. These stories are often used as tools for imparting wisdom to the younger generation.

Cultural Identity and Preservation:

Bhutanese folklore and myths play a crucial role in preserving the cultural identity of the nation. They are woven into festivals, dances, and rituals, keeping the Bhutanese heritage alive and vibrant.

Oral Tradition:

Traditionally, these stories have been passed down through oral tradition, with storytellers recounting them to captivated audiences. While written records have become more common, the oral tradition of storytelling remains an integral part of Bhutanese culture.

In conclusion, Bhutanese folklore and myths are an integral part of the nation's cultural tapestry. These stories connect the Bhutanese people to their land, their beliefs, and their values. They serve as a testament to the rich oral tradition and storytelling heritage that continues to thrive in Bhutan.

The Bhutanese Calendar and Festivals

The Bhutanese calendar and festivals are deeply intertwined with the country's culture, religion, and way of life. In Bhutan, time is not just measured in days and months; it's a reflection of spiritual significance and a way to celebrate the nation's unique identity. Let's explore the Bhutanese calendar and the vibrant festivals that grace this Himalayan kingdom.

The Bhutanese Calendar:

The Bhutanese calendar, known as the "Lunar Tibetan calendar," is a complex and astrologically significant system. It is based on the phases of the moon and is used in conjunction with the Gregorian calendar for administrative and business purposes. The Bhutanese year typically has 12 or 13 lunar months, and it can vary from the Gregorian year.

Losar - Bhutanese New Year:

Losar, the Bhutanese New Year, is one of the most celebrated festivals in Bhutan. It marks the beginning of the lunar year and usually falls in February or March. The festival is a time for families to come together, exchange gifts, and offer prayers for a prosperous year ahead. Elaborate masked dances and rituals are performed in monasteries across the country.

Paro Tsechu - The Festival of Masks:

Paro Tsechu is one of Bhutan's most famous festivals and takes place in the spring. It's a colorful and vibrant celebration featuring masked dances, known as "Cham," which depict stories from Bhutanese history and religion. Tourists and locals alike gather to witness this spectacular event.

Thimphu Tshechu - The Capital's Festival:

Thimphu Tshechu is the largest festival in the capital city, Thimphu. It occurs in the autumn and features religious performances, cultural displays, and traditional Bhutanese dances. The highlight is the unfurling of the Thongdrel, a large religious scroll, for the public to receive blessings.

Punakha Drubchen and Tshechu - Festivals in the Former Capital:

Punakha, the former capital of Bhutan, hosts two significant festivals. Punakha Drubchen is a unique festival that reenacts the 17th-century battle against Tibetan invaders. It's followed by Punakha Tshechu, featuring mask dances and religious ceremonies. These festivals honor Bhutanese history and spirituality.

Other Regional Tshechus:

Bhutan has numerous regional tshechus, each with its own distinct flavor and traditions. These festivals often showcase the local culture, history, and religious practices of the specific region.

Jakar Tshechu in Bumthang, Jambay Lhakhang Drup, and Wangdue Phodrang Tshechu are just a few examples of these regional celebrations.

Druk Wangyel Tshechu - Celebrating the Armed Forces:

Druk Wangyel Tshechu is a relatively recent addition to Bhutan's festival calendar. It was initiated to honor the Bhutanese armed forces and is held near the Dochula Pass. The festival features masked dances and patriotic fervor.

Haa Summer Festival - Showcasing Bhutanese Culture:

The Haa Summer Festival is a more recent addition to Bhutan's festival scene, designed to promote Bhutanese culture and traditions. It takes place in the picturesque Haa Valley and offers a glimpse into the rural way of life.

In conclusion, the Bhutanese calendar is a blend of lunar and Gregorian systems, but it's the festivals that truly define the passage of time in Bhutan. These vibrant celebrations, rooted in religion and culture, provide a unique window into the heart and soul of this Himalayan kingdom. Whether you visit during Losar, Paro Tsechu, or any of the other colorful festivals, you'll witness the Bhutanese people's unwavering commitment to preserving their rich heritage.

Learning and Understanding Dzongkha

Learning and understanding Dzongkha, the national language of Bhutan, is not just a linguistic endeavor; it's a key to unlocking the cultural and social intricacies of this unique Himalayan kingdom. In this chapter, we will delve into the fascinating world of Dzongkha, exploring its history, structure, and significance in Bhutanese society.

A Language Rooted in Tradition:

Dzongkha is more than just a means of communication; it's a symbol of Bhutanese identity. Its roots can be traced back to the 17th century when it was developed as the administrative language for Bhutan's government and religious institutions. Today, Dzongkha remains at the heart of Bhutan's cultural heritage.

Bhutan's Official Language:

Dzongkha is not only the national language but also the official language of Bhutan. All government and legal documents are written in Dzongkha, and it's the medium of instruction in Bhutanese schools.

A Unique Script:

Dzongkha is written in the Bhutanese script, which is known as "Uchen." It's a distinct script that sets Dzongkha apart from other languages in the region. Learning to read and write in the Bhutanese script is an essential part of mastering the language.

Challenges and Rewards:

For outsiders, learning Dzongkha can be a challenging endeavor. It's a tonal language with complex grammar and pronunciation rules. However, the effort is well worth it, as it opens doors to a deeper understanding of Bhutanese culture, history, and spirituality.

Language of Religion:

Dzongkha is intimately tied to Bhutanese Buddhism. Many religious texts and rituals are conducted in Dzongkha, and knowledge of the language is essential for monks and scholars. It's also the language of prayer and meditation in Bhutanese monasteries.

Preserving Linguistic Diversity:

While Dzongkha is the national language, Bhutan is a linguistically diverse country. There are numerous dialects spoken in different regions, and efforts are made to preserve and promote these linguistic traditions alongside Dzongkha.

Language as a Bridge:

For visitors to Bhutan, learning even basic Dzongkha phrases can be a bridge to connect with the locals. Bhutanese people appreciate the effort put into learning their language, and it can lead to more meaningful interactions and cultural insights.

Bhutanese Significance:

Understanding Dzongkha goes beyond practicality; it's a way to show respect for Bhutanese culture and customs. It's a tool for building relationships and forming connections in this close-knit society.

In conclusion, learning and understanding Dzongkha is a journey that goes beyond words and grammar. It's a gateway to the heart and soul of Bhutan, a nation that holds its language dear as a repository of its rich cultural heritage. For anyone seeking to truly immerse themselves in the Bhutanese experience, Dzongkha is the key that unlocks a deeper level of understanding and appreciation for this enchanting Himalayan kingdom.

Cultural Etiquette and Customs in Bhutan

Understanding cultural etiquette and customs is essential when visiting Bhutan, as it allows for respectful and meaningful interactions with the local population. In this chapter, we will explore the intricate tapestry of social norms and traditions that shape Bhutanese society.

Respect for Elders:

One of the fundamental principles of Bhutanese culture is respect for elders. When meeting someone older than you, it's customary to bow your head slightly as a sign of deference. This gesture is a way to acknowledge their wisdom and experience.

Conservative Dress Code:

Bhutanese people generally dress modestly. Traditional attire, such as the gho for men and kira for women, is the norm. When visiting religious sites, it's essential to dress conservatively, covering arms and legs. Additionally, hats and sunglasses are typically removed when entering religious buildings or homes.

Greetings:

The traditional Bhutanese greeting involves placing one's palms together in a prayer-like gesture and saying "Kuzuzangpo la" (hello) with a slight bow. Handshakes are also common, especially in more urban areas. When offering or receiving items, use your right hand or both hands as a sign of respect.

Religious Respect:

Bhutan is deeply rooted in Buddhism, and religious customs are highly respected. When visiting monasteries or dzongs, it's essential to show reverence. This includes walking clockwise around religious structures, not pointing your feet at religious objects or people, and refraining from loud conversations or laughter.

Photography Etiquette:

While Bhutan's landscapes and architecture are stunning, it's crucial to ask for permission before taking photos of individuals, especially monks or locals. Some monasteries may have restrictions on photography, so it's advisable to inquire first.

Eating Customs:

During meals, it's customary to wait for the host to start eating before you begin. Using your fingers to eat traditional Bhutanese dishes like ema datshi (chili and cheese stew) is acceptable, but it's essential to wash your hands before and after the meal.

Respect for Nature:

Bhutan is known for its pristine environment, and there's a strong emphasis on conservation. Littering is considered disrespectful and harmful to the environment, so it's crucial to dispose of trash responsibly.

Understanding "Driglam Namzha":

"Driglam Namzha" is Bhutan's official etiquette and dress code policy, which promotes the preservation of traditional Bhutanese culture and values. While visitors aren't expected to follow all aspects of "Driglam Namzha," being aware of its principles can help you navigate Bhutanese society with respect and understanding.

Hospitality:

Bhutanese people are known for their warm hospitality. When invited to someone's home, it's customary to bring a small gift, such as fruit or sweets, as a token of appreciation. Removing your shoes before entering a Bhutanese home is also a sign of respect.

Tipping:

Tipping is not a common practice in Bhutan, as service charges are often included in bills. However, if you receive exceptional service, a small gratuity is appreciated.

In conclusion, Bhutanese culture places a high value on respect, tradition, and spirituality. By adhering to these cultural etiquette and customs, you can forge deeper connections with the Bhutanese people and gain a more profound appreciation for the rich tapestry of traditions that define this enchanting Himalayan kingdom.

Bhutanese Music and Dance

Bhutanese music and dance are vibrant expressions of the country's rich cultural heritage. They play a significant role in religious ceremonies, social gatherings, and festivals, offering a captivating window into the heart of Bhutanese traditions.

Traditional Instruments:

Music in Bhutan is often accompanied by traditional instruments like the drangyen (a lute-like instrument), yangchen (a dulcimer), and the hauntingly beautiful sounds of the flute. These instruments create a melodious and soul-stirring backdrop to many Bhutanese performances.

Folk Music:

Bhutanese folk music is deeply rooted in the country's rural traditions. It reflects the daily lives, struggles, and joys of the Bhutanese people. Singers often use narrative songs to tell stories of love, nature, and local legends.

Religious Chants:

Buddhism holds a central place in Bhutanese life, and religious chants are an integral part of Bhutanese music. Monks and lamas use chanting to convey Buddhist teachings and perform rituals in monasteries and dzongs.

Masked Dances:

One of the most captivating aspects of Bhutanese culture is its traditional masked dances. Known as "cham," these performances are often held during religious festivals or tsechus. The intricate masks and costumes worn by dancers depict deities, demons, and historical figures. Cham dances are believed to purify the area, protect against evil spirits, and bring blessings.

Tshechu Festivals:

Tshechu festivals are celebrated throughout Bhutan and are characterized by colorful mask dances, traditional music, and religious rituals. These festivals are not only important religious events but also bring communities together for social bonding and celebration.

Modern Influence:

While traditional music remains deeply cherished, modern influences have also made their way into Bhutan. Contemporary Bhutanese music often incorporates elements of rock, pop, and hip-hop, creating a unique fusion of sounds. Young Bhutanese artists are increasingly blending traditional and modern music to reach wider audiences.

Bhutanese Dance Styles:

Bhutanese dance is diverse and encompasses various regional styles. The Cham dance, mentioned earlier, involves intricate footwork and graceful movements. Additionally, there are various other traditional dances like the boedra, zhungdra, and rigar, each with its own distinctive steps and costumes.

Cultural Preservation:

The Bhutanese government recognizes the importance of preserving its cultural heritage, including music and dance. Efforts are made to teach these traditions to younger generations through formal education and cultural institutions.

Bhutanese Artistry:

The artistry of Bhutanese musicians and dancers is celebrated not only within the country but also on international stages. Bhutanese performers often travel abroad to showcase their talents, sharing their unique culture with the world.

In conclusion, Bhutanese music and dance are vibrant expressions of the country's identity, deeply intertwined with its spiritual and cultural fabric. Whether it's the haunting melodies of traditional instruments, the mesmerizing masked dances, or the fusion of modern and traditional sounds, Bhutan's music and dance continue to captivate and inspire both its people and visitors from around the world.

Bhutan's Emerging Film Industry

Bhutan's emerging film industry is a testament to the country's commitment to preserving and sharing its unique cultural heritage with the world. While relatively young compared to the global film industry, Bhutanese cinema has made significant strides in recent years, drawing attention both locally and internationally.

Early Beginnings:

Bhutanese cinema began its journey in the early 20th century with the introduction of films by British political officers stationed in Bhutan. However, it wasn't until the 1970s that Bhutan produced its first feature film, titled "Gasa Lama's Blessing." This marked the formal beginning of Bhutanese cinema.

Unique Themes and Stories:

What sets Bhutanese cinema apart is its dedication to showcasing the country's rich cultural and spiritual heritage. Bhutanese filmmakers often choose themes rooted in Buddhism, folklore, and the daily lives of the Bhutanese people. The result is a cinema that offers a glimpse into the heart and soul of Bhutan.

Pioneering Filmmakers:

The Bhutanese film industry has been led by visionary filmmakers like Dzongsar Jamyang Khyentse Rinpoche, who directed the acclaimed film "The Cup" in 1999. This film, set in a Tibetan monastery in India, was Bhutan's official entry for the Academy Awards' Best Foreign Language Film category.

Global Recognition:

Bhutanese cinema has gained international recognition for its authenticity and unique storytelling. Films like "Travelers and Magicians" by Khyentse Norbu and "Vara: A Blessing" by Khyentse Norbu have been well-received at international film festivals.

Challenges and Growth:

Despite its cultural richness, Bhutanese cinema faces challenges typical of emerging film industries, including limited funding, access to international markets, and the need for modern filmmaking infrastructure. However, Bhutan's government has been supportive of its film industry, recognizing its potential as a cultural ambassador.

Film Festivals:

Bhutan hosts its own film festival, the Bhutan International Film Festival (BIFF), which showcases not only Bhutanese films but also international cinema. This festival provides a platform for emerging Bhutanese filmmakers to showcase their work and interact with the global film community.

Collaborations and Co-Productions:

Bhutanese filmmakers are increasingly collaborating with international partners to expand their reach and access resources for larger-scale productions. These collaborations have the potential to introduce Bhutanese cinema to a wider global audience.

Preservation of Culture:

Bhutanese filmmakers view their work as a means of preserving and sharing their unique culture with the world. Through cinema, they aim to bridge cultural gaps and foster a deeper understanding of Bhutan's traditions and way of life.

In conclusion, Bhutan's emerging film industry is a testament to the country's commitment to cultural preservation and expression. While still in its nascent stages, Bhutanese cinema has already made a significant impact on the global stage, and its future holds promise as it continues to tell stories deeply rooted in Bhutan's rich cultural tapestry.

Epilogue

In this epilogue, we reflect on the journey through the pages of this book, which has been a fascinating exploration of the Kingdom of Bhutan. From its breathtaking landscapes to its rich cultural heritage, from the unique Gross National Happiness Index to the traditions of Buddhism, we've delved deep into the heart of this enigmatic nation.

Throughout this book, we've learned about Bhutan's early history and origins, tracing its path from a collection of small fiefdoms to a unified nation. We've witnessed the profound impact of Buddhism on the country, shaping its culture, art, and way of life. We've followed the dynastic history of Bhutan's monarchs, witnessing their role in guiding the nation through periods of change.

We've seen how Bhutan transitioned to a constitutional monarchy, embracing democratic reforms while maintaining its unique cultural identity. We've explored the intricacies of its political structure, understanding how leaders govern while keeping the principles of Gross National Happiness at the forefront of their policies.

The chapters have taken us through Bhutan's economy, education system, arts, and cuisine, giving us a comprehensive view of life in this Himalayan kingdom. We've marveled at the country's unique architecture, exemplified by the dzongs that stand proudly in its valleys.

We've celebrated the festivals and traditions that bring Bhutanese communities together, highlighting the central role of religion in their daily lives. We've savored the flavors of Bhutanese cuisine, which offers a delicious blend of spices and local ingredients.

The chapters have also introduced us to Bhutan's incredible biodiversity, emphasizing its commitment to conservation efforts. We've embarked on virtual journeys through its national parks, getting a glimpse of the stunning landscapes and wildlife.

Bhutan's approach to sustainability and environmental conservation has left a lasting impression on us. Its dedication to preserving the environment while fostering economic development is a model for the world.

We've explored the country's remote villages and valleys, gaining insight into the daily lives of its people. The iconic Tiger's Nest Monastery and other sacred sites have taken us on spiritual journeys, understanding the significance of these places in Bhutanese culture.

The emerging film industry and Bhutan's unique postal service have showcased the nation's modernization while staying rooted in its traditions. We've admired its role in South Asian diplomacy and its efforts to maintain peaceful relations with neighboring countries.

Delving into Bhutanese folklore and myths has allowed us to appreciate the stories that have been passed down through generations. The Bhutanese calendar and festivals have given us a sense of the rhythm of life in this remarkable country.

Lastly, we've had a glimpse into the Bhutanese language, Dzongkha, and learned about the cultural etiquette and customs that shape interactions in the kingdom. Bhutanese music and dance have added vibrancy to our journey, and we've discovered the emerging world of Bhutanese cinema.

As we conclude this book, let us reflect on the magic of Bhutan, a nation where happiness is prioritized, where tradition and modernity coexist, and where the natural beauty of the Himalayas is a constant reminder of the wonder that is Bhutan. It is our hope that this book has brought you closer to understanding and appreciating the charm and complexity of the Kingdom of Bhutan. Thank you for joining us on this remarkable journey.

Printed in Great Britain
by Amazon